ENDORSEMENTS AND REVIEWS

Pre-publication review of *A God Beyond Belief*

Lance Moore has given us a lens through which we can better behold the complexity and wonder of an unfathomable God. His use of paradox takes us beyond the constraints of an "either/or" view to fully embrace a "both/and" God. A must read for our times as we seek unity out of coarse divisions.
Rev. Dr. Mark La Branche, President, Martin Methodist College

Praise for Dr. Moore's previous books

for *Outdoors with God:*
Reads awfully well ... a fine job ... a beautiful book in every way.
Pulitzer Prize winner Harper Lee, author of *To Kill a Mockingbird*

for *End of the World Propheteers*:
A masterpiece!
Rev. Dr. Thomas Lane Butts, author of *Tigers in the Dark*

for *Killing JFK: 50 Years, 50 Lies:*
Finally, a well-written, witty, and factual overview of the case that examines both the big picture and all the important details in the mosaic—without getting lost in a morass of tangential information. This is an important book. Not just "Recommended": Highly recommended!
Vince Palamara, author of *Survivor's Guilt*

for *Class Crucifixion*:
Timely, provocative, intelligent, well researched ... and entertaining. Whatever your personal politics, this book will interest you as it raises the level of debate above partisanship.

We believe it deserves a national audience.
www.FireTheRich.org

for *The Neurotic's Guide to God and Love*:
An interesting book by a talented writer. A treatise on love and grace, this helps counterbalance the 'Christians' who try to shame and blame folks.
James Wright, Environmental Attorney, Lakeland, Florida

A God Beyond Belief

Reclaiming Faith in a Quantum Age

A God Beyond Belief

Reclaiming Faith in a Quantum Age

Dr. Lance Moore

CIRCLE
BOOKS

Winchester, UK
Washington, USA

JOHN HUNT PUBLISHING

First published by Circle Books, 2019
Circle Books is an imprint of John Hunt Publishing Ltd., No. 3 East St., Alresford,
Hampshire SO24 9EE, UK
office@jhpbooks.com
www.johnhuntpublishing.com
www.circle-books.com

For distributor details and how to order please visit the 'Ordering' section on our website.

ISBN: 978 1 78904 254 2
978 1 78904 255 9 (ebook)
Library of Congress Control Number: 2018957353

A CIP catalogue record for this book is available from the British Library.

Design: Stuart Davies

UK: Printed and bound by CPI Group (UK) Ltd, Croydon, CR0 4YY
US: Printed and bound by Thomson-Shore, 7300 West Joy Road, Dexter, MI 48130

We operate a distinctive and ethical publishing philosophy in
all areas of our business, from our global network of authors to
production and worldwide distribution.

Contents

For Gaynor, who knew this book should be written.

Love is the Door, Humility is the Key.

Something Has Gone Terribly Wrong …

We face a spiritual crisis, but the extremes of Religious Fundamentalism on one hand, and Scientific Atheism on the other, offer no cure. Skepticism is soaring, especially among Millennials.

We daily read of scandals among our politicians, priests and Hollywood stars.

Mass shootings are epidemic, yet entertainment media glorifies violence.

Drugs, not "religion" as Karl Marx claimed, are now the "opiate of the masses."

"Christian" TV preachers use donations to purchase private jets and mansions — while children starve.

The White House has claimed that, "Truth is not the truth." Our leaders and institutions have lost all moral authority.

A common religious response to crisis is to thump the Bible harder and louder. This book challenges us to go beyond a simple, childish belief. The author offers an intelligent faith rooted in a respect for Scripture even while he takes a fresh look at calcified orthodoxies. He invites readers to **embrace paradox** — in Spirituality and in Science — to rediscover God for our Quantum Age.

An ordained minister with an unorthodox approach, **Dr. Lance Moore** is author of eight books, a six-time honoree for inclusion in the *Abingdon Preaching Annual,* and a repeat clergy panelist on Hallmark Channel's *Naomi's New Morning* with Naomi Judd. His book *Outdoors with God* received widespread praise, including this from the late **Harper Lee** (Pulitzer Prize for *To Kill a Mockingbird*):

"**Reads awfully well … a fine job … a beautiful book in every way.**"

An Un-skippable Preface

Beyond Belief: A Quantum God

Only the Paradox comes anywhere near to comprehending the fullness of life.
~ *Dr. Carl G. Jung*

This book is more about **religious paradox** than it is about science, so trust me, you don't have to know anything about physics to enjoy it. But like it or not, we now live in a "quantum age."

The Quantum View

December 14, 1900 marked a seismic shift in science. Launching us into the twentieth century with a bang, a fellow named Max Planck published a paper about how he had observed the universe in a new way. Quantum Theory was born. And everything changed.

How does a mere theory change the world? It seems more correct to say our cosmic *view* changed … but that's only if you don't see things with what I call "The Quantum View." Quantum Physics claims that *observing* something *changes* it.[1] Isn't it true that **the way we view life changes how we act**? Sooner or later, it does.

First example, Science: scientific theories — which are new ways of viewing the natural world — yield technologies that transform society. The microwave oven wasn't life-changing, but the atomic bomb sure was.

Second example, Religion: via "The Book of Mormon," Joseph Smith came up with a new way of viewing Christianity, and two centuries later, it changed the kind of underwear Mitt Romney uses.[2]

But seriously, folks ... the dramatic advances in science over the last century contributed to the steep decline of Christianity in Europe.3 Similar decline in American religion has been slower in coming,[4] but one thesis of this book is that **traditional orthodoxy must grow (or die) in the face of expanding knowledge.** Picturing God as an enthroned old man with a white beard is no longer satisfying for a scientifically-minded generation. Paradoxically, I am also arguing that intelligence is *not* a measure of faith. We must go beyond a childish belief and accept that science has validity; we also know that faith requires us to go beyond scientific materialism.

Beyond Belief ... Embracing Paradox

Now is the time to reconsider both long-standing Christian orthodoxy, and classical physics' orthodoxy, to adopt a "quantum way" of viewing reality — and God. We will return to the phrase *Quantum View* in a moment, but centuries before that phrase was coined, these concepts were foreshadowed in the idea of *paradox*.

A brief definition of paradox is "a statement that seems absurd or contradictory, yet may be true." It comes from two Greek words: *para* ("beyond or contrary to") and *doxe/dokeo* ("belief, opinion or expectation") — and is an interesting contrast with the word *orthodox*. **Paradox is a key to understanding the mysteries of a quantum-acting, infinite, complex God.** Orthodoxy (a word we shall parse later) claims to be "The Truth." But I'll argue that the unresolved paradox is the only form of full truth available to mere mortals (even the truth of Scripture must be understood utilizing paradox). If we rush to grasp just one side of a paradox, we have a half-truth. And a half-truth can be as damaging as a lie.

The *Paradox Paradigm* ... and Other Fun Words

Each chapter herein is framed around a particular paradox. The chapter titles use a symbol — the Greek letter *Chi* "χ" — to present the two sides of each paradox as a **connected tension** (rather than an oppositional "vs."). Another way to put it: the chapter themes are not *This versus That*, but are presented in the form *Topic A* is in a Paradox with *Topic B*.

Use whatever words you wish: a chiasmus, parallelism, matrix, or juxtaposition. I love words ... if you don't, then feel free to skip ahead to Chapter One. Or dig deeper. Consider the word *paradox* and its synonym, **juxtaposition**. The latter emerged in French from the word *position* ("a point of view on an issue"), added to Latin words meaning "beside, closely connected, or joined." From Jerome's Latin Bible, the same root word (*iugum*) behind *juxtaposition* translates as "yoke" in the English Bible. And a paradox can be two contrasting ideas that are *yoked* together. I share this to remind us of Jesus' fondness for parables and paradoxes, as when he said: "My yoke is easy and my burden is light."[5] His metaphor compares a master's connection with his disciple-servant to a plow "yoked" with an ox. Benevolent farmers made sure the yoke fit comfortably on the animal's shoulders, and did not overwork the ox. Jesus rebuked religious leaders for overburdening people with strict laws,[6] so his yoke analogy was in answer to that: his yoke is light, easy and "fits well."[7]

Jesus also associated the yoke with *learning*: "Take my yoke upon you and learn from me ..."[8] Living with and learning from paradox is not unlike wearing a gentle yoke. It may sound like a silly tongue-twister, but Jesus offered a new **paradigm** based on **paradox** and taught in a **parable**.

Othodoxy and ... Is Paradoxy a Word?

Remembering that the Greek prefix *para* means "throw beyond," I write about "paradoxy" in order to "go beyond" the way we approach belief and *orthodoxy*.

[Note: I am using the word "orthodox" to refer generically to "orthodox Christianity," not to the *Greek* or *Eastern Orthodox*

Church.]

Orthodoxy means "correct doctrine, approved opinion, or right teaching," a word assembled from Greek and Latin words for "right, straight, correct" and "opinion, teaching." This begs the question of *who* **gets to determine** *which* **doctrine is correct.** Aren't most Scripturally-based orthodox teachings in dispute by one church, sect, preacher, imam, guru, or another? Who is correct … and why?

Take for example the Scriptural command, "Thou shalt not kill." Everyone agrees that's a good and reasonable prohibition. Yet, are there not contradictions and exceptions surrounding that Commandment? Sure, killing is a bad thing. But don't we kill (execute) serial murderers? Don't we kill "enemies" in a war? Regardless of my personal feelings about the sanctity of life, I cannot deny that good folk argue this principle of "Thou shall not kill" quite differently depending on the situation. Puzzlement and paradox abound.

The Big Bang Theory … and Reality

When I write of our *quantum age*, I'm not referencing so-called *New Age* Eastern Mysticism (the New Age fad peaked in the Eighties). Quantum Science is substantial, not just abstract or mystical, and from the start, was not merely a hypothetical theory. When Max Planck (mentioned in the first paragraph) began this new field of physics, he proved his ideas with actual experiments. He showed that energy can exhibit characteristics of physical matter — even before Einstein confirmed it with his famous formula, $E=mc^2$. Planck coined the term *Quanta* (from Latin) to describe energy particles. Previously, classical physics had defined light energy only as a wave, but the new quantum view found that light can be a wave **and/or** a particle. Other physicists, like Niels Bohr, would use the word *paradox* to help understand these new, quantum, "either/and" concepts. The complexities of physics are explained best using paradox and parable ... just as with religion.

In turn, the Big Bang Theory of our cosmic origin seems to have substantial evidence for its reality, yet paradoxically, it in no way rules out that God was the Creator behind the "bang." When it comes to considering the moments before the creation event, the Big Bang no more explains where the primordial "stuff" came from than does Genesis explain where and how God pre-existed.

Quantum Connections

Quantum physics, does, however, *sound* a lot like a mystical religion. In 2015, Jennifer Oulette *wrote* an article intriguingly entitled "Spooky Quantum Action Might Hold the Universe Together," examining why many physicists believe the universe consists entirely of tiny particles (*quanta*) glued together by **Quantum Entanglements** — unseen and distant quantum connections that bind reality in a cosmic tapestry. Her interviewees emphasized that the universe is far more complex than scientists envisioned just decades ago. We've long known that a small lump of gold, for example, is comprised of billions of atoms. But when I was a school kid, teachers told me that the element Gold (Au) was a "simple" atom made of circling electrons, protons and neutrons. Now we know there is nothing simple about it. At the sub-atomic level, the particles and movements that determine the metal's characteristics are of exponential complexity.

The physicists in her article strained to find words to convey the intricacy and numbers represented in even a single crumb of reality. All of this brings to mind these words of Jesus: "If you have faith as small as a mustard seed, you can say to this mountain, 'Move from here to there,' and it will move. Nothing will be impossible for you."[10] We thought Jesus was using hyperbole. Turns out he was grossly *under*stating. The numbers involved in determining the makeup of a grain of mustard seed (the charges, spin direction, form and location of quanta, etc.) would require enough hard-drives to fill our entire **galaxy**, according to physicist Brian Swingle.[11] And we have learned that a spoonful of plutonium can literally move a mountain. Yes, Jesus was speaking of the power of faith, but he simultaneously reminded us how small our imaginations can be and how immense a speck of Creation is. I don't think Jesus would be at all uncomfortable in a room full of physicists discussing the universe in quantum terms!

Beyond Voodoo

Years ago, when I first read about "The New Physics" and tried to explain *Quantum Entanglement* to an intelligent friend, he exclaimed in amazement: "That can't be true ... that's like voodoo stuff!" People scoff at Bible stories about a tempting serpent, a talking donkey and a floating zoo. But the truth is stranger than any fairy tale. Those odd Bible stories are neither the source nor the problem with Belief (most are metaphors, not meant to be history or science lessons). **The problem is not our belief, but our limited imagination.** Belief is only a baby step; true faith must go beyond belief.

God Is BIG

So, any aim of this book is to argue for an expansion of our narrow understanding of God. In 1953, J. B. Phillips did not exaggerate when he entitled his provocative book, *Your God is Too Small*. The Bible portrays an infinitely-larger God than the bearded One inked in the "Christian comic book" lessons that I read in Sunday School as a kid. Scripture describes One who is "hovering over the face of the deep," casting uncountable stars across the cosmos, transcending past, present and future. In Acts 17, the Apostle Paul told the Greek scholars that God encompasses *all* existence ... he said we float in God, we live and breathe and have our being within God's vastness. Theologian Paul Tillich built upon that, calling God "the Ground of All Being." It's not Star Wars pop philosophy of "The Force" permeating all things; it is traditional, orthodox Christianity: all things exist within God. Thus, the beautiful, endless Creation reveals the character of our Creator.

This is why I speak of a "Quantum God" who is BIG (like a *quantum leap*, as used in pop lingo), ACTIVE, and exponentially COMPLEX. Scriptures portray God as the infinitely creative hand, always moving. From my faith perspective, God *is* the "quantum action" behind cosmic phenomena small and large — both the sub-microscopic sub-atomics, and the gargantuan spinning galaxies. When physicists write about entangled particles not bound by the limits of chronological time, I think of Scripture describing God as existing "yesterday, today and tomorrow," and of Jesus' words: "Before Abraham was, I am." When we read of a cosmic Big Bang explosion of light and energy, I hear Genesis: "In the beginning, God ... said, 'Let there be light.'" And I remember the Book of Job describing God as the one who "brought forth the constellations and bound the chains of the Pleiades."

Holistic vs. Dualistic

As we close this wordy Preface, allow me to identify one more aspect of the Quantum View: it approaches things **holistically**, rather than with a black 'n white dualism. Early classical physics, much like primitive Western religions, viewed most things in terms of dichotomies: hot-cold, light-dark, up-down, yes-no, positive-negative. By contrast, quantum physics tends to view things "in living color," so to speak — relationally and holistically, in 3D *gestalt*. Quantum physicist David Bohm suggested that the universe is made of holograms, and without going into a science lesson above my head, he meant that each part of the hologram contains all the data of the whole hologram. So, Bohm said, "Everything is in everything." That's mind-boggling ... I don't understand it, and I'm not even sure if his theory is true. But it reminds me of these Scriptures: God "made known to us the mystery of his will ... to be put into effect when the times reach their fulfillment — to bring unity to all things in heaven and on earth," and "Christ is all, and is in all."[12] Everything in everything.

I am asking us to risk opening the gateways of our minds, hearts and spirits to reconsider a big, complex, quantum-acting God.

Chapter 1

The Paradox of Knowledge χ Innocence

God commanded: "Of every tree of the garden thou may freely eat; [except] the tree of the knowledge of good and evil, thou shalt not eat of it ..."
~ *Genesis 2:16–17, KJV*

How long, you simpletons, will you insist on being simpleminded ... how long will you fools hate knowledge?
~ *Proverbs 1:22, NLT*

The clash between the verses above (Genesis vs. Proverbs) is enough to confuse any religious seeker. Should we seek knowledge ... or not? I have an answer. In fact, if you wanna know the secret knowledge of the universe, I'll tell you how to find it: *Embrace Paradox.*

Paradise Lost, Paradox Found

We all desperately seek happiness, the *dolce vita,* the good life. Many of us seek salvation or enlightenment, to boot. We desire the knowledge of good and evil and more. We want these things, we suspect they require some sort of surrender or sacrifice ... yet we do not want to lose our innocence, our freedom or our *identities*. Our desires are mired in paradox. We want to have our cake and to eat it, too. And what good is cake if we can't eat it?

Another secret is, ironically, that **simple belief is not enough**. Knowledge alone is not enough. Paradise is not found in facts and figures; merely "believing in God" is a meaningless expression. Adam and Eve believed in God, and even gained "the knowledge of good and evil." But what happened? Paradise was lost!

Here in this post-modern era, we need more than a fairy tale belief *and* we need something more than an outdated scientific framework. We need to revisit stale, petrified orthodoxy — whether it be scientific orthodoxy or religious literalism (see more on those topics in Chapter 3). We need a new paradigm. So, I propose the Paradox Paradigm.

The Thorntree in the Garden

Let's back up. As Julie Andrews sang in *The Sound of Music*, "Let's start at the very beginning. A very good place to start." As a child, I wondered why, in the biblical Creation story, Adam and Eve were given the entire Garden of Eden, yet were forbidden from grabbing hold of the "fruit of the knowledge of good and evil." Whether you view Genesis as a literal history of creation, or as Myth, it is still True in the greater sense.[13] The truth about this "knowledge of good and evil," this *gnosis*[14] thing, seems to be connected with our entire **purpose**. We were exiled from Paradise into a thorny garden called Earth. Why?

Maybe to learn something ... and like Dorothy in Oz, "you have to learn it for yourself," over time. Enlightenment, the secret gnosis, can't be handed to you like ruby slippers or snatched from an apple tree. Which brings us to restate a key paradox: "Knowledge is Both Good and Evil." Without the proper experience, context and humility, knowledge can be as dangerous as ignorance. This seems to be the lesson in the Garden of Eve story, as well as in the ancient Greek myth of Pandora's Box.

Pandora's Paradox

In one version of the story, Prometheus stole fire from heaven (the fire also being a metaphor for Knowledge/Gnosis). The god Zeus sought revenge by giving a jar or box to Pandora, the wife of Prometheus. Zeus commanded her not to open it — knowing full well that curiosity would get the best of her! Her world-changing disobedience and curiosity echoes Eve's biting of the apple; in Greek mythology, Pandora was the first human, just as Eve is the first human in Judeo-Christian tradition. Eve brought the Curse and Sin upon humanity; Pandora's Box unleashed sickness, death and all the other evils of our world. In both stories, God/Zeus did not restrain Eve/Pandora, hinting of a plan to ultimately bring something salvific out of the tragedy. In the Bible, God promised Eve that she would give birth to a savior (albeit generations later in Jesus). Pandora quickly closed the container, but only one item remained: Hope. Pandora's Box and Eve's Paradise are parables teeming with the paradox of tragedy and hope.

Underlying the stories of Adam/Eve and Prometheus/Pandora is the idea that when humans receive anything from God, it comes with a consequence. God wanted to share the miracle of existence, to place us in Paradise, but in allowing us full, sentient existence, the gift of Knowledge and Free Will allowed evil to enter the world. Like Genesis, Pandora's Box conveys an enigmatic truth about the human condition. Hope remains, but the path back to Paradise is riddled with thorns.

And riddles.

The Purpose of Life

These mixed metaphors tell us that Life is a tribulation. So, what is the purpose of such a life? From my Christian perspective, I believe it is found in three things:

1. **Love.**
2. **Service to others.**
3. **Personal growth that comes from the long *struggle* of love and service.**

Salvation usually comes not in any single "Eureka!" moment. It takes time. Instant gnostic enlightenment is fool's gold. Experience and growth cannot be imparted through words on a page. We are stuck with words. And as Joseph Campbell argues in his book, *The Power of Myth*, "Story" can convey more than mere words. So, here's another story:

Life's Vital Struggle

As kids, my best friend Billy and I were avid butterfly collectors. Surprisingly, no one beat us up for being sissies as we ran around our small town with pastel-green butterfly nets. Billy was a tough guy. He would grow up to be a medical doctor, maybe because he tried performing surgery at 13. Our surgical patient was a cocoon. We had found the large cocoon and knew from our collecting studies that it would "hatch" into a beautiful Polyphemus moth — a moth as big and iridescently gorgeous as the better-known Swallowtail butterfly. We kept the cocoon in a glass jar all winter. At last the day came for the caterpillar-reborn-as-moth to emerge, and we were there to observe. After initially poking its head out of the paper-like shell, it seemed to us the moth had become stuck, unable to extract itself. So, Billy the eager surgeon took an *Exacto* knife and carefully sliced open the cocoon, freeing the moth. Then to our disappointment, the moth's wings remained flaccid. The wings never unfolded, never gained turgidity, never spread out the metamorphosed beauty ... and never flew. Our Caesarian Section caused a premature birth that short-circuited the transformation process from worm to flyer. Without the struggle of stretching and climbing from the chrysalis, the moth never became the exquisite creature nature intended.

Do I need to explain the moral of the story? Hopefully it's obvious. Giving Adam and Eve the instant fruit of gnosis without any struggle was like freeing a moth too soon.

The Paradox of Adult Knowledge and Childlike Innocence

In case you haven't noticed, *Paradox* is the overarching theme of this book. The paradoxes come straight from the pages of

Scripture, including this one: **How can we move beyond a simplistic, literalistic childish religion, yet keep the open-arms faith of a child?** The answer begins with recognizing the difference between *childish* vs. *childlike*. Child*ish* belief is whimsical, sentimental and fleeting. You can't build a life on it ... it is the foundation of sand. Mature faith has a solid foundation of logic and experience, yet a grown-up faith still should be child*like*: open-minded, unbiased, pliable and curious. The prophet Isaiah urged us to strive for intellectual growth, saying things like: "Come now, and let us reason together, saith the LORD ..."[15] When Jesus directed us to "become like little children" in order to enter the Kingdom of God (or, if the reader prefers Eastern language, to *receive enlightenment*), he was not contradicting Isaiah. Scripture often seems to contradict itself, but with patient study, the conflicts enrich our understanding. The Bible encourages us to have an innocent, childlike faith, **and** to develop a thoughtful, mature faith — to "walk with the wise and become wise,"[16] to use our God-given brains. Jesus himself had "grown in stature and wisdom." Paul encouraged spiritual seekers to grow beyond "babies' milk."

If Only Things were Simple ...

A puzzle still remains in this. The Bible warns that "the reasonings of the wise" are "useless." Jesus praised God for having "hidden these things from the wise and learned, and revealed them to little children." He said we must "change and become like little children." Strange advice, it seems, since any god who could create a universe would be smarter than all our Einsteins, Hawkings and super-computers put together. Why would the Creator of the Universe ask us to dumb-down our spiritual understanding?

God doesn't. God did not make religion simple. Those who believe that Scripture is "God-breathed" (i.e. *inspired*, if not written directly by God) must therefore admit that God **allowed** the many paradoxes (what some call "contradictions") in the Bible (or other holy scriptures, if your faith background is not Judeo-Christian). "Why?" My thesis is that there is a grand purpose in this. Once we become open to seeing the paradoxes found in Scripture, we can then pursue a deeper understanding of a complex God for Quantum Times.

Keeping Scripture Relevant

My message is **not** that the Bible is outdated. However, our interpretation of it may be. Many of us grew up with a one-dimensional, sentimental "ole time religion," and we're hesitant to admit that it might be limiting the breadth and power of Scripture. In our technological age, a great problem with both Islamic and Judeo-Christian fundamentalism is a failure to explore the complexities of faith, and a great reluctance to adapt to seismic social shifts. Does 2000-year-old orthodoxy help us, or hinder us, in seeking a multi-faceted God whose intelligence makes a super-computer seem like an abacus? 5000-year-old scriptures had already told us that God looms ubiquitously beyond the limits of time and space. Now we know the cosmos is a million times more complex than the ancients could have imagined. So, the term *Quantum God* seems apt. The word *quantum* is used paradoxically in English, referring both to the tiniest, sub-atomic particles, *and* for something astronomically big (*e.g.,* "a quantum leap").

Paradox and the Seven Deadly Sins

Rushing to resolve (or avoid) a paradox ... could that be a sin of laziness, impatience or arrogance? Early Christian teaching cautions us against those two famous *Deadly Sins*: Sloth and Hubris (Ego-Pride). Mindless allegiance to an inflexible, one-dimensional orthodoxy from our childhood: Is that not Slothfulness? And I ask myself, "Am I arrogantly holding on to *MY* faith or *MY* god as a personal, private base of authority and dominance?" Humility begins by saying: "I don't own a monopoly on truth; I can't fathom all the mysteries of God."

The Book of Job, the oldest book of the Bible, is a curious tale of Satan's assault on a hard-luck fellow named Job. His three "friends" stand by and watch his calamities, only to lecture him with pious platitudes. In the end, God admonishes their weak theology and intellectual laziness, taunting them: "Where were you when I laid the earth's foundation? Tell me if you understand ... Can you bind the chains of Pleiades ... or loosen Orion's belt?"[17] A fair summary of God's lecture to Job might be: *Who do you think you are? How dare you put simple words in My mouth? How dare you think you know even a fraction of the things that the Universal Creator knows — the One who spun the stars into constellations, made planets out of nothingness!*

The Sin of the Smug

So, the message of Job is not just a "theodicy" sermon about why suffering exists.[18] It's a warning against **theological smugness**. Job's haughty friends were trying to reduce infinite wisdom down to a few clichés. Pardon me for sounding smug and judgmental myself, but maybe the pious literalist should swallow Job like a pill: a corrective for self-satisfaction and self-righteousness.

If we reduce Scriptural truth to a facile, one-sided theology, are we not guilty of doing what Job's friends did? This is not so much a paradox as it is an irony: fundamentalists who revere Scripture often ignore the very words — holy words — which warn them against narrow literalism and reductionism. Job's friends were convinced they were holy and wise. They believed they not only lived the righteous life, but also had the divine truths memorized into pithy, concrete aphorisms. God said no.

Purpose-Driven Life, Revisited

Returning to the question of "Purpose": Over 30 million people have purchased Reverend Rick Warren's bestseller, *The Purpose-*

Driven Life. Those book sales show that people are hungry to know life's purpose ... and Pastor Warren has some helpful things to say on the topic. However, I take pause when he describes a reality in which everything, in every moment, is micro-managed by God. In a book with a rejoindering title — *The Reason-Driven Life* — Professor Robert Price rebuts such "Pre-Destination Theology," arguing convincingly that Warren's assumptions are built upon selective Bible reading. Predestination leads some to ask: "Okay, if God is controlling *everything*, am I just a robot? I might as well quit all efforts to do good, to learn, to work ... and just take a long nap."

After my 60 years of observing the harsh reality of human existence, I cannot picture God as a micro-managing puppet-master. Who can accept the idea that Pain and Evil are God's Desire for us? Predestination Theology, taken to the extreme, leads to blaming God for all things. In 2013, Rick Warren's precious son, Matthew, died —a tragic suicide due to mental health issues. To his credit, Rick has not impugned God nor abandoned his faith. I greatly respect Pastor Warren. But I wonder how his theology deals with such tragedy and loss. Are mental health issues and suicide part of "God's eternal purpose for each life"? Warren's writing success stems partly from his admirable ability to make things clear and concise. **But life is rarely clear and concise.**

Truth and Mystery

This is not to say that Truth requires intensive scholarship and intellectualism. *Some* basic aspects of faith and reality are truly simple. Four things I know to be true are:

God is Love.
God Saves.
God is Truth.
God is Paradox.

That last thing is a Mystery, something that cannot be fully known or understood. Yet it is absolutely true. That, too, is a paradox. How can I claim to "know" truth while asserting that Truth = Mystery?

The Quantum View and the Paradox Paradigm

This is not a book about quantum physics. This book is about God. To better know God and God's cosmos, I cite quantum theory for a reason: Quantum Physics demands we accept the reality of paradoxes — two facts that appear to be in opposition or that logically cannot exist simultaneously, and yet *are* co-existent and linked.[19] Quantum mechanics may ultimately confirm that Paradox is woven into the very fabric of the universe.[20] My use of phrases like "Paradox Paradigm" and "Quantum View" are more than mere buzz words. These phrases represent **tools**. Or consider them like a pair of spectacles: the Paradox Paradigm and the Quantum View are frames with a pair of lenses that can help us view the divine mystery, a way to glimpse an infinite God with our finite mind.

Projecting Our Dumb Humanness onto God

Genesis 1:27 states that we were made "in the image of God." Don't reverse it. Don't try to make God into *our* image. Anthropomorphizing (projecting our human character and foibles onto God) causes us to underestimate God's infinitely high IQ. Some Christian readers may resist the phrase, "a high-IQ God," hearing in it some sort of pseudo-intellectual, New Age attempt to enshrine intelligence. I am not a New Age Gnostic, seeking salvation through secret knowledge. I am a "traditionalist" in this regard: the Bible describes God as "love," and that is far more important to me than the quantum-level intelligence of God.

The same is true for us. The human heart is more vital than

brains, metaphorically speaking. Smarts alone are not enough. To receive full truth, we also need creativity, openness and innocence, which is what Jesus meant in saying we must "change and become like children."[21] That remark from Jesus is **anti-egoism**, not anti-intellectualism. Babies have no ego ambitions. Jesus' words were a call to surrender ego. Consider his further teaching: "Whoever humbles himself as this little child is the greatest in the kingdom of heaven."[22]

The Smartest of Times, the Dumbest of Times

We live in paradoxical times in terms of *human* intelligence. Technology, computers, scholarship and research have expanded the available knowledge of our species to, well, *quantum* levels; yet the masses are dumbed-down by fluffy pop-media that cater to the lowest common denominator. "Reality" TV shows impart "wisdom" from a six-year-old Honey Boo Boo — famous for saying, "Farting helps you lose weight." (A straight line can be drawn from the airing of the "Here Comes Honey Boo Boo" show in 2012, to the reality show, "The Apprentice," to the election of President Donald Trump in 2016.)

I will argue that, contrary to popular thought, the decline of spiritual fervor in America **stems not from a lack of emotion, but from a lack of rationality**. I have an emotional love for God, but it is my knowledge/reason that keeps me fervently faithful when feelings wax and wane.

Summary

The biblical command to reject "the wisdom of the world" is not asking us to close our minds; rather, it is a call to reject those things in our society that are misguided, in favor of seeking bigger, higher, cosmic Truth. It is time to explore the mysteries and complexities of faith, to adapt to a changing civilization, and to seek a quantum God whose intelligence is beyond our science.

Unfortunately, misinterpretation of Scripture has fed

a strand of anti-intellectualism among some Conservative Evangelicals. This has contributed to the decline of Christianity in advanced countries. Church attendance has wilted in Europe, and mainstream Christian denominations are in a slow death-spiral in America. That decline is driven by a loss of confidence in Institutional Religion, *and* a loss of confidence in Spirituality. For too long, the Church has skirted around, covered-up or rationalized away the many contradictions in the Bible. Other religions make similar mistakes. Whenever we find two contradictory ideas from the same Bible (and this may be true for scriptures of other religions, too — especially Zen Buddhism), the ideas ultimately may not conflict. They may be two sides of the same coin of understanding.

To repeat and summarize: this book proposes a new way to approach these so-called contradictions. For fun, I call it the Paradox Paradigm. Another way to put it: Embrace *unresolved paradoxes*. As stated in my Preface, **the unresolved paradox is the only form of full truth available to humans**. To receive and partially understand one is not the same as trying to prematurely resolve it. If we reject the part of a puzzle that makes us uncomfortable, we have a distorted picture, a half-truth. Sustained paradoxes are best handled when we blend higher intelligence *with* a "heart faith." Some use the phrase *blind faith*, but I would prefer to speak of a faith of head and heart and will: an open-eyed, conscious yet humble acceptance of the divine mystery. This too is a paradox.

The opening quote for this chapter (from Proverbs 1) may strike some readers as insulting. I don't like to be called a "simpleton" or a "fool." But if we misinterpret Jesus' command to become childlike, we probably *are* being simpleminded. The same Bible that teaches us to have the innocent humility of children *also* instructs people of faith to "walk with the wise and become wise" (Proverbs 13:20), "to add to your faith goodness ... and knowledge" (2nd Peter 1:5), and generally encourages us to use our God-given brains, as with Isaiah's order: "Come now, and let us reason together, saith the Lord."[23] I pray this book offers a positive direction for twenty-first-century spirituality. So, I challenge believers and doubters to go deeper into the truths of God and of the Universe, to have the courage to "open Pandora's Box," to face the full conundrum of Quantum Faith.

Questions for Thought, Study and Group Discussion

The author states: "The purpose of life is found in three things: love, service to others, and personal growth." Do you generally agree, or would you word it differently? More personally, would you be willing to share how you define your own specific life-purpose?

Does our Purpose, within the phrase "service to others," include Christ's "Great Commission" to go and teach others of the faith? If so, would a follower of another religion be receptive to that?

~Express your own understanding of the author's assertion that "the unresolved paradox is the only form of full truth available to humans." Do you agree, or is this an overstatement? Explain/discuss.

Paradox 1

Knowledge can be both good and evil. Without experience, context and humility, knowledge can be as dangerous as ignorance.

Reflective Quote for Chapter 1

A little learning is a dangerous thing; Drink deep, or taste not the Pierian spring. ~ *Alexander Pope, Poet,1709*

Chapter 2

The Paradox of Grace χ Law

It cannot be said too often that in the New Testament, the opposite of sin is not virtue, it is faith.
~ Robert Farrar Capon, in Kingdom, Grace, Judgment: Paradox, Outrage, and Vindication in the Parables of Jesus

Life is strong and fragile. It's a paradox ... It's both things, like quantum physics: It's a particle and a wave at the same time. It all exists all together.
~ Joan Jett, Rock Star

Life is a paradox. And that's saying more than just, "Life is an enigma or puzzle." **A paradox can be an *answer*, not just a puzzle.** The cartoon character, Bart Simpson, was asked by his teacher to employ the word *paradox* in a sentence. Unsure of the exact definition, Bart *ad libbed*, "Uh ... Damned if you do, damned if you don't!" The teacher begrudgingly admitted that Bart had answered correctly.

To-Do Lists: From Alpha to Zen

All great truths are wrapped in paradoxical tensions, from Astrophysics to Depth Psychology to Zen. The Judeo-Christian religion, in particular, wrestles with *Bart's Paradox* ... with several ways of being damned by doing, or not doing, certain things. The Jewish religion had elaborated a detailed "to-do list" in order to save us from damnation. It was so punctiliously rigid no one could live up to it. The barbarians populating much of the Old Testament couldn't even spell *punctilious*, much less obey an encyclopedic list of *dos and don'ts*.

I am far from the first to write about this. In the so-called

"Patristic Age" (circa 100–450 CE), the monastic Early Church Fathers and Mothers withdrew into cloisters to free themselves from the material world, to avoid temptations of the flesh and to devote themselves to spirituality. But even when they succeeded in living virtuously, a problem arose. Many discovered that they would then fall victim to the sin of Hubris. For the virtuous nuns and monks, it may have been hard to escape feeling spiritually superior toward those outside their sacred walls — thus becoming guilty of excessive Pride. This is yet another form of Bart's Paradox: **the harder we work at becoming righteous, the more self-righteous and egotistical we may become.**

Ignoring the futility of "salvation by works," the early Roman Catholic Church tried an end-run around the conundrum: they suggested one could buy his/her way to sainthood via *Indulgences* (cash paid to the church). The Protestant reformer, Martin Luther, perhaps short of cash, had sought to *earn* his way into heaven by making a holy pilgrimage to Rome. He spent hours prayerfully knee-climbing a marble stairway in the Vatican, until finally he heard the chastising voice of God saying, "The righteous shall live by faith." So, Luther saw the folly in all of it, stood up, and rebelled against Catholicism's emphasis on "salvation by works." Luther went back to study Paul's writings on the Grace vs. Law problem, and could only conclude, like Paul, that he must "live by faith" — *faith* meaning a trust in Grace, not Law. He tried, with some success, to embrace the grace and forgiveness side of the "sin paradox." But Luther never fully resolved the Grace vs. Law dichotomy, as he could not escape traditions that were bound up in his own ego.

Angel Wrestling

Long before Luther's time, the patriarch Jacob had his own encounter with a "stairway to heaven." The Torah relates how Jacob had a dream or vision of angels descending heaven's ladder. Then he wrestled all night with an angel (or was it a demon?),[24] trying to gain God's blessing. It finally came ... as a paradox. Accompanying the blessing, Jacob was cursed with damage to his hip socket and a painful limp. Spiritual growth usually comes after painful wrestling.

As one of the first Jewish-to-Christian converts, Paul had wrestled mightily with *Bart's Paradox*. In the same epistle where Paul advised the church in Rome to live by faith alone, he confessed: "In my inner being I delight in God's law; but I see another law at work in the members of my body, waging war against the law of my mind."[25] Paul had found himself a "prisoner" of the paradox, *wanting* to do right, but unable to do so. Theologians call this problem by various names, using dualistic phrases such as Law vs. Mercy or Works vs. Grace. But such *Dualism*, labeling things as simply *this* vs. *that*, leads us astray.

Dualities lead to reductionism. Over-simplification. Either/or thinking. With Dualism, we settle too quickly on one side, discarding the other, thus losing the value of the original paradox. Theologian Richard Rohr understands the danger. Rohr wrote: "If you can hold and forgive the contradictions [i.e. paradoxes] within yourself, you can normally do it everywhere else, too. If you cannot do it in yourself, you will actually ... project ... dichotomies everywhere else."[26]

Dichotomies tend to go hand in hand with demonization — labeling the other as "the Enemy." Such a black or white, good or evil, nothing-in-between judgmental dualism is exactly what Jesus railed against. As mentioned above, the early patristic literature is filled with cautionary lessons against judging others while self-smug.

Modern religion isn't handling dualism very well. This may manifest as outward condemnation of others, or alternately as an inward, personal feeling of "damned if you do, damned if you don't." American churches, at their worst, can be dualistic and have settled on one side of their dichotomies (Baptists and

Fundamentalists on the side of rigid Law; Liberals on the side of a cavalier devaluing of Law/Scripture). Denominational, doctrinal fights are like the common occurrence in court cases. Two honest witnesses of the same crime describe different events because of where they stood in viewing the event and their own assumptions and prejudices. I'm suggesting that any future success of faith (for both organized religions and personal spirituality) will only come for those who are able to shift their viewing perspective; only those who are willing to surrender an ego-need to be "absolutely right" and examine their own biases have any hope of finding truth. Surrendering ego does not mean going to the other extreme, it does not require giving in to the "other side's" biases. It is achieved by **living with paradox and viewing life and faith holistically.**

A Good Man Is Hard to Find

The last half-century has been a period of disillusionment. We've learned that many of our TV preachers, Hollywood celebrities and Presidents had secret sexual sins. Too many CEOs have been exposed as greedier than King Midas. Thousands of priests have been found guilty of perverse abuse of children (assisted by bishops and cardinals who covered it up); since 2004 alone, the Vatican has sanctioned or defrocked over 3000 priests.[27]

In elementary school, I was taught about the noble heroism of our Founding Fathers; they were certainly brave, but they also owned (and in some cases, molested) slaves. The historical list of "sinners" seems to be predominately male — but in many cases, there were women complicit as well. Assuming Eva Braun never raised any moral objections to Adolf Hitler's atrocities, was she any less guilty than her husband? Diogenes, the Greek Cynic, went about holding a lantern to the faces of Athenians, claiming he was searching in vain for an honest man. A perfectly good woman may be just as scarce.

We "religious folk" like to think we are on a stairway to

heaven, a path to righteousness. Maybe so. But living out an authentic faith is hard, and it can be just as frustrating with organized religion as without it. Doctrinal religion demands we be morally good, but religious history recounts more moral failure than success.

Morality Machine?

All have sinned and fallen short. Maybe we should give up Temperance for Lent. One cause of the decline in Christianity's share of population in the northern hemispheres is our fixation on religion as a morality machine. A friend of mine, raised in the Southern Baptist tradition, remembers church as mostly oppressive — a place where the pulpiteer "always seemed mad at us," where "Sunday School was a course in dos and don'ts ... but mostly don'ts," and where dressing in nice clothes seemed more important than caring for others.

In my youth, our congregations were exclusively Caucasian, because church-decreed morality did not include racial justice. The Methodist Church that I attended as a child emphasized Grace more than the neighboring Baptist Church did; nevertheless, when the threat of Sixties integration loomed, some of the "Christians" in our Alabama church informed the Methodist pastor (my dad!) that "If any Blacks try to come sit in our pews, we plan to meet 'em at the door with a baseball bat." They likely used a different term for "Blacks," and I don't mean Colored. (I'm proud to say my father stood up to the bigots and chastised their lack of Christian love — resulting in the bishop moving us to another city.) If religion was a morality machine, it had engine failure.

The Radical Jesus

Read the New Testament. It has no "Ten Commandments," is one-third the length of the Old Testament, yet still employs the words "Grace" and "Forgiveness" over 150 times. Jesus repeatedly challenged the notion that religion should coerce folks into perfect rectitude. Jesus warned: "And you experts in the law, woe to you, because you load people down with burdens they can hardly carry, and you yourselves will not lift one finger to help them."[28]

Paul also fought against legalism, and urged us not to be crammed into conformity: "Do not let the world squeeze you into its mold, but instead let yourself be transformed by the renewing of your mind."[29] The context of that verse was Paul's plea for us to rely more on Grace and less on religious legalism. Yet to this day, seekers become disappointed and disillusioned if they don't fit the mold. They join a church to meet Jesus and to find his promised peace, but then collide with judgmental leaders who load them down, demanding unrealistic perfection. (Later in this book we will examine whether Jesus' phrase "Be ye perfect ..." is often grossly misinterpreted.)

Of course we need moral standards, and children certainly need to be taught not to lie, steal and kill. But let's be honest: most well-intentioned adults do not benefit from an ongoing guilt trip or shame complex. As a PK (Preacher's Kid) myself, I can tell you that as many or more preachers' kids became rebels as became saints. Speaking of physics: the normal reaction to excessive pressure is an explosion.

It seems unfortunate that the entry level for most Christians, or for any religion, is "moral self-improvement." That is not an attractive feature of religion. The elementary notion of "religious = do-gooder" is not much different from when I joined the Boy Scouts and swore to their motto, "Do a Good Turn Daily." There's nothing wrong with that, nothing bad about seeking Merit Badges in Scouting and Gold Stars for church attendance and striving for a moral life. But it is a limited first step, not meant to be a resting place on our life journey toward full maturity.

Über Boy Scouts?

Like other spiritual leaders and prophets, Jesus calls us to climb higher, to seek a "higher righteousness" — but he also knew how daunting that call is, especially when it is misunderstood as hyper Boy Scoutism. So, he was quick to accept and forgive his followers when they failed. When Jesus spoke of perfection of thought and action, he was pointing to a future goalpost, an ideal destination. Personally, I doubt he expected us to reach perfection in this lifetime. Even John Wesley, who demanded that his Methodist ministers attain "perfection in this life," viewed this "higher righteousness" as more of a higher spirituality than as a spotless résumé. Confusingly, while calling for perfection, Wesley conceded that "... there is no such perfection in this life, as implies an entire deliverance, either from ignorance, or mistake, in things not essential to salvation, or from manifold temptations ...", and he went on to say, "I do not contend for the term *sinless* ..."[30]

It's notable that all the non-divine characters of the Bible were flawed — many of them downright scoundrels — and never came close to matching the ideal Christian portrait that Jesus modeled. Even when Bible "heroes" seemed to have become "holy," they later became guilty of spiritual pride or moral failure: for example, read about Noah's drunken night; or about Abraham the bigamist, offering his wife to another man to save his own skin; or Jacob stealing Esau's birthright by deceiving a blind man; or Samson's vengeful killings; or David's adultery and murder of Uriah; or Solomon's greed and sex addiction that rivaled Hugh Hefner (1st Kings 11:3: "He had 700 hundred wives ... and 300 concubines ..."). Within the much smaller cast of the New Testament, we still have Peter's denials/lies, the petty jealousy and infighting amongst the Disciples, Paul's history of stoning folks, etc. Even Judas the greedy betrayer started out as one of those "good guys" of the Bible!

The Self-Righteous Trap

To repeat: Paul, St. Augustine, and Martin Luther are but a few of many "religious heroes" who came face-to-face with this paradox of righteousness: even *when* they managed to go a day free of sin, the resulting spiritual pride became a sin of its own. Folks whose dispositions and circumstances *do* make them comfortable as moral Puritans can quickly fall into a trap of self-righteous egoism. This is a second, negative paradox within the first: we need religion to help us find our spirituality, but the practice of religion sets up barriers to belief.

I am still a fan of "The Church," convinced that a fulfilling life of faith comes to those who seek the help of a loving fellowship, a community of believers. In our jaded era, it is hard to convince people that an organized practice of faith and a systematic theology are good things. Studying the past experiences and accumulated wisdom of seekers before us can help us find a way out. Yes, even something as dry as "church history" can guide us.

Breaking Out of the Vicious Circle

So how do we escape the vicious circle? If arrogance is the problem, and I think it is, what unlocks the chain?

Humility is the key. Why did Jesus spend so much time modeling humility if not to teach us emphatically that humility is the Way? He didn't come incarnate as an infant in a manure-strewn barn just so we could set up cutesy, sentimental manger scenes. (And don't get me wrong; I enjoy nativity scenes.) He was teaching us the very essence of how we ought to be. He didn't "model" servanthood and humility to look good, like a New York fashion model; he modeled humility by embodying the Sacrificial Servant's life and death, in order to teach us how we are to live.

The escape path out of the paralyzing circle of sin, hubris and guilt is a path through Paradox itself. The path of humility, open-mindedness and **self-surrender** (more on that topic later) is blocked by fear. Fear stops us. For some, it is a fear of hellfire. For others, it is a fear of being "soft on sin," or "Liberal," or an agent of Satan. Ask yourself: Was Jesus lying when he said repeatedly, "Fear not!"? 1st John 4:18 flatly asserts: "There is no fear in love." Fear clouds the truth, limits our progress on the path of spiritual maturity, robs us of enlightenment ... whatever metaphor you wish to use, fear keeps us imprisoned and burdened. (We will examine that paradox in a later chapter.)

Love is the only antidote for fear and guilt. Jesus said, "The truth shall set you free." His definition of "Truth" is nearly synonymous with "Love and Grace" (see the famous verse, John 3:16, for example). Love can set us free. Consider whatever burden you are carrying. What is it doing to you? Wouldn't you like to get rid of it? Would you like to be free?

Saying Grace

So many books, sermons and essays have been penned on the meaning of *Grace*, I hesitate to add to the verbiage. The classic Christian definition of Grace is "God's love and forgiveness, given to us without regard to our merit or goodness." Christians sing about this *Amazing Grace*, yet find it hard to accept the gift.

I love the old hymns, but one line of another hymn is disconcerting: "'Are ye able?' said the master, 'to be crucified with me,'" and the chorus answers, "Lord, we are able!" As for moral perfection, I'm **not** able, and doubt very seriously you are able, so let's quit pretending. Let's quit laying burdens on people that we ourselves can't carry. Don't let go of the paradox of Law and Mercy: The Law points us toward an ideal morality, a goal to strive for; the Grace saves us from despair and rebellion. Moreover, once we admit we "aren't able" and that we must depend upon Grace, we could be inoculated against Spiritual Pride. Don't brag about a God-given, God-paid-for righteousness.

Grace is free. In Romans 6:23, Paul states it plainly: eternal life is "the gift of God." A **gift**. Free, from God. In that same verse, Paul refers to the "wages of sin," so the contrast between *wages* vs. *the gift* is clear: forgiveness and the ensuing eternal life (what Christian's term "salvation") is *not* earned, it is a gift. Trying to live the good life is not how we earn Grace, it is how we *respond* to Grace. Good deeds are how we thank God for the freedom given us. Jesus wants us to rise above selfishness and to "crucify" ego, to empty our hate by being filled with love. But Jesus knows we can do none of it by human effort alone.

The Ragamuffin Gospel

The late Brennan Manning was a priest, best known for his bestselling book, *The Ragamuffin Gospel*. Manning taught, preached and wrote emphatically that Jesus' message is primarily one of grace. He found it impossible to earn salvation by being a goody-two-shoe; instead, Manning found working with recovering alcoholics and addicts more refreshing and authentic than dealing with the pretenses of a parish. Manning preached from a heart of true humility, and reminded us that God's plan is easily misconstrued in our society. Manning lamented that all too many Christians focus on comfort and material luxury even as we seek to please God in the most superficial of ways, "as though the Almighty is only a small-minded bookkeeper" who tallies sins only to use the tally against us. Manning found such a god foreign to his experience of an all-loving, all-forgiving God.

One of Manning's students was the award-winning Christian musician, Rich Mullins. Mullins wrote these words:

Jesus said, "Whatever you do to the least of these my brothers you've done it to me ..." [So the best way to follow Jesus] is to identify with the poor. This will go against the teachings of all the popular evangelical preachers. But they're just wrong. They're not bad, they're just wrong. Christianity is not about building an absolutely secure little niche in the world where you can live with your perfect little wife and your perfect little children in a beautiful little house where you have no gays or minority groups anywhere near you. Christianity is about learning to love like Jesus loved ... and Jesus loved the poor and Jesus loved the broken-hearted.

Mullins lived out his belief: his songs sold millions, which could have made Rich *rich*. But Rich Mullins gave away the bulk of his music profits and lived like a pauper, by choice, on an "Indian Reservation," where he taught music to Native American children until his untimely death in 1997. His music, teaching and life example actually makes me question my own claim that no one is able to live a pure, perfect Christian life. Mullins came close.

Summary: The Paradox Should Remain

I do not wish to overstate or to argue so forcefully for the supremacy of Grace that it violates my own plea to resist "resolving paradoxes" or settling on just one side of the equation. Law — moral codes and standards written in Scripture — has its place. If we make no attempt or intention to do what is good, right and true, we have no love in us. Morality does matter. The Law points us to righteous behavior. The Law gives us boundaries and guidance, which is something humans need, to say the least.

As stated before, our behavior (attempting to follow a moral law) is the proper response to grace. While an earlier quote from the 1st Epistle of John testifies to the grand gift of love and grace, it also reminds us that God's gift should engender reciprocity in us: "Since God so loved us, we also ought to love one another." And "This is how we know that we love the children of God: by loving God and carrying out his commands."[31]

Questions for Thought, Study and Group Discussion

Has this chapter helped you view the tension of Law and Grace in new ways? If so, try to vocalize your thoughts on it.

When is church attendance and membership a help and joy for you? When is it a burden?

Which seems easier for you, loving the Unseen or the Seen? Loving God, or showing your love for God by loving your neighbor?

Jesus asks us to be perfect. Do you think he meant in this life? Or only as an ideal for the next life? How might a person live out Christ's call to "a higher righteous"?

Paradox 2
If we succeed at goodness and altruism, we then run the risk of spiritual pride. But we should keep trying.

Reflective Quote for Chapter 2
For by grace you have been saved through faith, and this is not your own doing; it is the gift of God — not the result of works, so that no one may boast. ~ *Ephesians 2:8–9 (NRSV)*

Chapter 3

The Paradox of Divine Scripture χ Human Writing

> You study the Scriptures diligently because you think that in them you have eternal life ... yet you refuse to come to me to have life.
> ~ *Jesus, in John 5:39–40*

> [W]hile Scripture may be inerrant, there are no inerrant interpreters of Scripture.
> ~ *Wendy Vanderwal-Gritter, New Direction Ministries of Canada*

Jamie Coots was, literally, killed by literalism. Rev. Coots died of multiple rattlesnake bites in the middle of his church service.[32] His church is nestled in a valley of the Cumberland Mountains, in Middlesboro, a Kentucky town whose claim to fame is its location inside an enormous meteorite crater. Coots had accepted Scripture as literal truth, including Mark 16:18: "They will pick up snakes with their hands ... [and] deadly poison ... will not hurt them at all." He made the mistake of taking a Scripture that was partly metaphorical and limited to a particular point in time (intended to give hope during extreme Christian persecution), then applying that one obscure verse improperly: as literal and universal. Coots is not the first religious "snake-handler" who has died because of a poor understanding of contextual Scripture.

Literalism and Inerrancy: Time-Out for an Old Debate?

Biblical *Literalism* and biblical *Inerrancy* are two different but closely-related ways of viewing Scripture. Literalists are reluctant to view Scripture metaphorically or in a cultural context. The

34

definition of "Inerrancy" varies, but Wikipedia's definition is a good starting point: *The doctrine that the Bible is without error or fault in all its teaching.* Literalists tend also to believe in biblical Inerrancy, and the most stringent insist that every single letter in the Bible comes from God and demands unqualified acceptance. Together, these views result in an inflexible approach, at times giving too much emphasis to what may be "minor" verses. This issue has been debated for centuries; in our "Quantum Science" era, time has run out on their logic.

This chapter's argument is twofold:

1. Literacy and Inerrancy have serious logical problems.
2. Approaching Scripture from those viewpoints leads to difficulties for faith adherents. For example, in Islam, how would a fundamentalist Muslim reconcile Qur'anic verses on *jihad* ["... slay them wherever ye catch them ..." (Al-Qur'an 2:191)] with verses that teach mercy and peace ["... take not life, which God hath made sacred ..." (Al-Qur'an 6:151)]?[33] For Christians, love, acceptance and tolerance are often casualties for those with a Literalistic, and especially Old Testament, approach. If you find yourself strongly disagreeing with that assessment, and thus are tempted to discard this book, prove you are "accepting and tolerant" and give my case a fair hearing. Pray for an open mind.

A personal note: Let me here state that I do believe the Bible is divinely inspired and authoritative for my faith. I treat the Scripture with care and reverence and even take issue with some "liberal" scholars who sow doubt about the words of Jesus. I believe Jesus actually said the things the gospel writers reported! So please do not dismiss this sincere consideration of how we might best approach the interpretation and understanding of Scripture.

Religious *Practice* Reveals Ideology?

In the South, we don't see this bumper sticker as often as in my youth: "The Bible said it, I believe it, that SETTLES it!" The ultra-strict defenders of Inerrancy and Literalism are in the minority of Christendom, as most of us have the more reasonable understanding that Scripture cannot be "perfect" as long as it is conveyed by imperfect human language to imperfect eyes and ears. Scripture must be read in context and interpreted wisely. Generally, people are aware that careful study of the Bible, and a wider contextual interpretation, are prerequisites to understanding.

And yet, a large number of otherwise intelligent believers *function* as if they were strict Bible literalists. Their actual, pragmatic approach reveals a narrow view of metaphor. Even the most open-minded of us may yet be constricted in our daily religious practice, because at a gut level we still yearn for a simple, matter-of-fact instruction manual for life. Face it: **The Bible is not that.** It is *not* simple. Scripture is complex, symbolical, metaphorical and — my favorite word — *paradoxical*. If you were to focus on a single verse for guidance in the face of a challenge, you would be missing a fuller understanding, and perhaps be making the wrong choice, by ignoring a contrasting verse.

The Literal Truth and Nothing but the Literal Truth?

Our biases tend to push us toward a single perspective. Intentional open-mindedness requires we push back. Consider the possibility that there is more than one way to view Truth. For example: Yann Martel's book (and movie), *Life of Pi*, ends with the narrator, Pi, inviting the listener to choose which version of his life story to accept as truth. He had told two tales of his life: one version magical and wonderful but hard to believe, the other story edgy and unsatisfying yet easier to believe. Pi's patient listener was calm, rational and scientifically minded; yet, faced with the two versions, the listener chose to accept the fantastical one. The listener still expressed to Pi his frustration in being left with uncertainty, having to take the story on faith. Pi answers: "So it goes with God."

Anyone who thinks God has given us a definitive, one-sided, absolute story is not in touch with the depth — and paradox — of Scripture. Those who reduce God's truth to bumper sticker maxims are guilty of *idolatry* — not much better than those who take the infinite, mysterious God and shape "Him" into a clay figurine placed on the mantle so they might have a palpable god. And behind many denominational and sectarian doctrines is the sin of *pride*. It is the ultimate arrogance to think that MY denomination exclusively has the complete understanding of the infinite God.

So far, this book may trouble fundamentalist Christians; they may be labeling me a "Compromiser," "New Ager," or "Liberal," when I am none of those. I'm not even part of the "Emergent Church" movement (although I am sympathetic with many versions of the Emergent Church, and I've seen that movement unfairly maligned as a "counterfeit religion"). To repeat: my devotion to God, my respect for Holy Scripture, my refusal to cherry-pick verses and my caution in misusing the word of God, plus my veneration of martyrs, my appreciation for the teaching of the monastics, my belief in the mystical ... in all these things, my background is as a Moderate, even Traditional, Christian. But ...

This Is Where You Lose Me

Where I part ways with modern American religion is when it reeks of cocksure authoritarianism. Ecclesiastical authority is a form of **power**, and **power corrupts**. There's no way to say this without sounding both critical and condescending, but the egoism and power-mongering found in the hierarchies of even the more moderate denominations is terribly troubling. I recognize such Egoism because I've come to know it in my mirror.

The sin of hubris in literalism is revealed when a pastor or bishop (or emphatic layman, for that matter) declares that only *his* experience, *his* context, *his* understanding of language, is the Right One (yes, I say "his" because it tends to be males who run these institutions). I have observed persons' well-being sacrificed on the abstract altar of "Church Law."

We must admit this: thousands of different "Bible churches" and "Bible teachers" espouse their own monopolies on truth. Surely the problem with that is obvious. *Monopoly* means only one out of many ... and yet, religion has a hundred different "monopolies." The late Herbert W. Armstrong was quite emphatic that his "Worldwide Church of God" was the only True Church; the Jehovah's Witnesses were emphatic that only their 144,000 true believers would be in heaven; before Vatican II reforms, Roman Catholics were ardent about their monopoly on truth; ditto the bombastic, self-righteous radio and TV preachers; and so on. The problem in claiming to have the One True Church or One True Creed is that it means you're calling everyone else wrong. I'm not sure how to say they were *all* wrong without being guilty of hubris myself. But maybe they were. All wrong.

All wrong? I do not mean wrong on *all* of their beliefs or teachings. But every one of us has probably been wrong on at least *one* point of doctrine or practice. It is certainly wrong to assert that "my church" has the one and only Absolute Truth, the One True Religion. We may be able to state a clear, concise Creed — but how could that pin down the Infinite God, and how could that Creed even mean the same thing for all its adherents? Even within a specific denomination and a single congregation reciting the Apostles' Creed on Sunday morning, the two hundred congregants have two hundred different perspectives on what those words mean for each of them. I do believe Jesus is *the way, the truth and the life* ... but on any given Sunday, a thousand different preachers could deliver a thousand different sermons on the meaning of that New Testament verse. So personally, while I believe in God as an Objective Absolute Truth, do I really know more than a fraction of it? We will revisit this point in a later chapter. For now, let's agree that humility is called for. With that said, consider further the question of Literalism and Inerrancy.

Is Scripture Perfect?

The Bible is amazingly trustworthy — usually self-consistent, and 99 percent accurate "typographically," so to speak, as later manuscripts are nearly-identical with older ancient manuscripts. The scribes were extraordinarily meticulous. The events of the Old Testament connect or mesh with events in the New Testament (Christians view Jesus as the fulfillment of Jewish prophecies of the Messiah). These features make the Bible unique among religious documents. Written by over 40 authors across centuries, in three different languages, the Bible maintains an enviable consistency and textual reliability, and its number of ancient extant manuscripts exceeds all other religions' texts combined. The Bible is rather unique among ancient texts in the way it came to be written, assembled, canonized and confirmed.

But as any Bible with footnotes will tell you, the manuscripts are *not* 100 percent perfect. Manuscripts do differ. Defenders of the Bible are quick to point out that the textual variants between, for example, *Codex Sinaiticus* vs. *Codex Vaticanus*, do not alter the overall message. It seems, however, that since we have no single manuscript (and certainly not an "original copy") of the entire Bible that perfectly matches another ancient manuscript, calling the Bible "inerrant" is a poor choice of words. Even something as slight as a different spelling in Manuscript A vs. Manuscript B still constitutes an "error." So, in plain fact, the Bible is NOT inerrant.

The Bible is still relevant, holy, special, unique, and wise ... but it is not inerrant. If God had been concerned about having a

100 percent perfect, flawless version of Scripture, God could have presented us with inscribed tablets. Or with iPods containing a God-narrated Audible book. God chose not to do that. (Islam's Muhammed and the Mormon's Joseph Smith both claim that angels gave them heavenly-written golden tablets, but the tablets are no longer extant and there were no other witnesses to the angels' visits.) No, God sent the Bible piecemeal over thousands of years, via flawed human prophets and scribes and even a few scoundrels, mostly recorded on damaged papyrus, using a variety of human languages that don't easily translate into clear English.

Some Famous Inconsistencies

More than mere spelling differences, the Bible has some (though surprisingly few) irreconcilable inconsistencies with itself; Scripture contains violations of scientific facts and laws. Though the apologists for inerrancy make feeble defenses, several outright contradictions are well known. For example, 2nd Samuel 24 and 1st Chronicles 21 record the same event: King David gave a royal decree for Joab to take a census of the kingdom. But there are clashing differences: Samuel's version states that **God** "incited" David to order the census; Chronicles states that **Satan** incited David to order the census. The apologists try to claim that God used Satan to incite David ... but that would require a loose addition or metaphorical interpretation to change the actor/inciter from God to His opposite, Satan — the very kind of "looseness" with Scripture that the Bible literalists decry! Moreover, 2nd Samuel and 2nd Chronicles report different numbers of fighting men of Israel and Judah. No small error: their numbers are off by hundreds of thousands. The better "inerrancy scholars" do not even try to claim these were different events. Instead, their explanation relies on this kind of weak, strained logic: "It could be that the author of 2nd Samuel was indicating the number of 'seasoned veterans' when it referred to 'valiant' men, while the author of 1st Chronicles was numbering *any* man who drew the sword, not just the valiant ones."[34] So we are expected to believe that an ancient census that counted over a million men — without calculators or any easy-to-use census recording instruments — took the time and effort to record *which* soldiers were "valiant" and which ones weren't? Nothing in Scripture even hints this was the case, as the word *valiant* is not even defined or explained in the context.

The Bible Is Not a Science Textbook

The controversies over Creation, Evolution, and the Book of Genesis have been so thoroughly discussed, debated, spindled and mutilated, I have little desire to further decimate forests by spending more than a page on the matter. "Young Earth Creationists" are technically correct in pointing out that geological dating is educated conjecture; dating by rock strata and via Carbon-14 is good science, but not a *precise* science.[35] But don't pretend the Bible is precise, either. A lack of precision in Science or in Scripture actually doesn't matter when it comes to belief in a divine Creator. Whether our planet is four billion years old or just a million or less is not determinative in the questions of evolution or whether God is our Creator. God could have created us in seven days, or space aliens could have accelerated the evolutionary process, or God could have used evolution as a "slow tool" for creating life. We really can't prove (beyond a shadow of a doubt or to the exact day) events that may or may not have happened before written history. My faith is not dependent on science, geology *or* on Bible literalism.

Let's be honest: most educated persons will not accept every detail of the Noah's Ark story at a literal, matter-of-fact level. "Creationists" seem compelled to insist that the story is true, citing geological evidence of a giant flood, and the fact that a similar story, the Gilgamesh/Babylonian flood epic, is an "outside source" that confirms the tale. Science agrees there were ancient catastrophic floods (when the glaciers melted, for example), and I don't have a problem believing that Noah (or Gilgamesh) had a vision from God to build an ark to save his family from a regional, or wider, flood. But to accept the full Genesis story at face value, as some Fundamentalist's do, requires an exercise in mental gymnastics. Frankly, it demonstrates the intellectual self-deception of Literalists. And it weakens Christianity's credibility. Here's why.

Here Comes the Flood

Genesis tells us that the Ark was to be a floating "Bed 'n Breakfast" for "... two of every kind of bird, of every kind of animal and ... every creature that moves along the ground ..."[36] "Every living thing that moved on land perished — birds, livestock, wild animals, all the creatures that swarm over the earth, and all mankind."[37] Pairs of all of these creatures, plus ample supplies of seeds and spores to replace all plant life, plus eight humans, plus enough food and supplies to keep them all fed and happy for a **year**[38] — these all would need to fit within one boat less than half the size of the Queen Mary.

To keep things simple, we'll set aside the whole question of mass genocide and destruction by a god who sounds more like Hitler than Jesus. We will also set aside the question of how Noah "rounded up" the animals, because Genesis says they would "come to Noah" on their own (in other words, the text explained this as a miracle of God). So, let's just consider the impossible claim that all those animal pairs, with a year's supply of food, would fit into the primitive ship. Scientists have made a conservative estimate: 10,000 different bird species x 2 = 20,000 birds (including flightless emus swimming in from Australia, and the dodo bird, not then extinct); 10,000 mammals; 16,000 reptiles/amphibians; 2 **million** insects and remaining categories ("creeping things").

How do the defenders of Inerrancy answer this? They claim

that the biblical word, "kind," does not mean "species." So instead of having to take two polar bears, two grizzlies, two brown bears, etc., Noah just boarded a single bear species ... implying that the other species later evolved from those two parents. But wait: The Literalists don't believe in Evolution. Oops. So, they actually answer with, "This isn't evolution, it is normal genetic variation."[39] Ask a geneticist about that claim. A distinct-species polar bear existed centuries before even the oldest-claimed biblical dates for Noah's flood (a fossilized polar bear jawbone has been dated to over a 100,000 years prior to Noah, and DNA studies indicate the species is more than four million years old!).[40] And this claim that "kind" only referred to a select few species is in direct contradiction to what the Bible *literally* stated, repeatedly, in Genesis 6 and 7: that "every" creature on earth (other than fish) died. Thus, they all needed an ark.

So, we have established that for the Bible to be true, either:

A: A pair of polar bears swam/walked from the Arctic to Mesopotamia, a 6000-mile journey.

Or B: God magically "transporter-beamed" the polar bears to the Ark. However, the Bible is quite specific in mentioning/ identifying miracles in every other occasion, but says nothing of the sort in the Flood account.

Or C: The Bible story is metaphorical or allegorical, not literal.

Which seems more likely?

The Day the Sun Stood Still

Still not willing to reconsider Literalism and Inerrancy? Examine this: in the Book of Joshua, the Israelites were battling the Amorites, and Joshua prayed to God to extend the daylight in order to finish slaughtering their enemies. So, the Bible reports, "The sun stopped in the middle of the sky and delayed going down about a full day."[41] We will yet again set aside the questionable portrayal here of a vengeful God who "hurled large hailstones down" upon the Amorites, killing more of them by God's hand than were "killed by the swords of the Israelites."[42] For our purposes, this is a question of scientific accuracy. The Sun does not revolve around the Earth, thus cannot be "stopped in the sky" to extend the length of a day. Perhaps the Earth could be miraculously stopped from turning on its axis in order to extend the day's length. But that is not what the Bible says, and if God were concerned about the Bible being perfectly "inerrant," why would the Lord not inspire the writers to word things accurately?

Psalm 104:5 similarly presents an ancient writer's primitive view of a non-spinning planet: "He set the earth on its foundations; it can never be moved."

A literalistic reading of these passages violates what every sixth Grade science student knows: the Earth spins, creating day and night ... the sun does not actually move "across the sky" or around the Earth. If the apologists for Inerrancy Doctrine wish to claim, "This is poetic language," or "This is a product of the limited view of ancient man," then they are agreeing with my very point: the Bible comes to us from specific places, times and cultures, using human language and understandings that in turn must be taken into consideration when we interpret its meanings for our life and times.

What Does the Bible Claim for Itself?

Does the Bible even claim Inerrancy and perfection for itself? Not really. The conservative literalists base their claims for that on a handful of verses, none of which are as specific or emphatic as they pretend. The chief New Testament verse (in 2nd Timothy) asserting that Scripture is inspired by God does not address the issues of scribal accuracy or absolute perfection of manuscripts at all. It vaguely states: "All scripture is inspired by God and is useful for teaching, for reproof, for correction, and for training in righteousness."[43]

Compare that to this description of Christ himself, in 1st Peter 1:19: "... a lamb without blemish or defect." Jesus is described as **perfect**, free of flaws; Scripture, however, is merely described as "inspired" by God, not as a stenographer's court transcription. In contrast to how Jesus is described, the Bible never calls itself perfect or free of defect. Yes, Jesus did make the oft-cited "jot and tittle" statement about Scripture: "Do not think that I have come to abolish the Law or the Prophets; I have not come to abolish them but to fulfill them. For truly I tell you ... not the smallest letter [jot], not the least stroke of a pen [tittle], will by any means disappear from the Law until everything is accomplished."[44] But in that very same homily, Jesus actually *did* overturn the Law. He fulfilled the requirements of the Law, via Grace, thus changing the Jewish Law. For example, Jesus emphatically abolished the rule of "an eye for an eye." Thus his "jot and tittle" statement could not have been an endorsement of Scriptural Inerrancy. It was something of a hyperbolic, illustrative statement showing his respect for Scripture, to prepare his audience for what he was about to do. Immediately alongside that statement, Jesus made some controversial additions, interpretations and changes to the Torah. Scripture will endure forever; however, its *application* dramatically changed with the coming of Christ.

The same goes for Paul: he respected Scripture, yet he did not enshrine it as an idol or employ it as a magic incantation. Paul asserted that his epistles were "by the word of the Lord" (1st Thessalonians 4:15) and God's message was "revealed by the Spirit to His holy apostles and prophets" (Ephesians 3:5). That is far from making claims that some sort of magical protection kept Scripture free from mistranslation or misinterpretation. In fact, two thousand years of Christian history shows that millions of smart, sincere Christians have each arrived at different conclusions as to the meaning of various Scriptural principles.

God Is Perfect; Scripture Is Imperfect

What the Bible *does* say is that we should not label anyone or anything as perfect, other than God. The Bible is not perfect. Jesus said only God is good/perfect.[45] To claim otherwise is to argue with Jesus, and to break the Commandment against idolatry. We worship a living God, not an old parchment. Scripture is inspired by God, but the Bible is NOT God; we do not bow down and worship words on paper. This may sound irreverent or disrespectful of Scripture. But it is a necessary corrective. If we make an idol out of "the Good Book," we disobey its very words.

Anyone who has studied the history of the making of the Bible should honestly admit that Scripture has its limitations. Calling the Bible "inerrant" or "infallible" requires mental gymnastics to defend. If God somehow magically protected "His original words" to the level of perfection, why did God allow so many different manuscripts to have variants? Despite the diligent care and reverence that the Jewish Scribes and Christian monks took in transcribing Scripture, across the generations a few errors did indeed occur.

Other than the ten sentences brought down from Mount Sinai on stone tablets by Moses (now lost to history), the Bible was not handed to us in a FedEx package from God. The making of the Bible was a process that resembles **evolution** more than it does an instant, "created in six days" miracle. It was crafted slowly — over centuries — with human hands holding crude human writing instruments, using finite human language. Inspired by God, yes, but still reliant upon the written word, and the humans who conveyed it were caught within the limits of their primitive cultures (their *Sitz im Leben*).

An Important Caution

Allow me to clarify: I am not attacking the overall value and truth of Scripture. I am not calling Genesis "a myth" in the sense of an imaginary fairy tale. To repeat: the question is not "Is Scripture trustworthy?"; the issue is "How do we best understand the truth of Scripture?" It is *not* paradoxical to believe the Bible is a true narrative even as we distinguish between styles of writing. What parts of the Bible are symbolical, metaphorical or figurative speech, and which parts are literal histories? Are parts of Scripture a news story or a science textbook, or something else? Those questions are not conflicting at all.

While I push against some aspects of Literalism and Orthodoxy, I resist any atheist who might condescendingly dismiss Scripture because it has a few fantastical events. The vast majority of serious scholars of the Bible, both secular and sectarian, find it to be profound and sophisticated overall.

For example, the important truths in the Creation story still hold up well in our times: an eternal God created the universe *ex nihilo*, out of nothing. That's a sophisticated concept to have emerged from a primitive culture in the days of Job and Genesis. Quantum physicists can't explain where the "stuff" of a Big Bang came from, and the deeper they peer into the makeup of matter, the more it resembles "nothing." It is more accurate to describe atoms as being the result of waves of vibrating energy than to say they are made up of solid bits and pieces![46] Atoms do *not* have a physical structure as Democritus the Greek — and many a schoolteacher — taught us. Genesis 1:3 states that God "spoke" and the cosmos was created out of a void, and Job 38:7 adds that during the act of creation, "… the morning stars sang together and all the angels shouted …" Thus, the biblical version of creation is not only more sophisticated than many (more than one religion starts their creation myth with a giant tortoise),[47] it is also not a far stretch from the scientific reality that all existence is made up of vibrating frequencies — of which, audio energy (whether God's speech or the music of the spheres) is an analogue.

Summary

With that said, we can't escape the fact that ancient human

language doesn't hold up well when it comes to the more detailed facts of science. Let History instruct us here. In the Middle Ages, most Christian "scholars" ardently insisted that the earth was flat and the sun, stars and planets circled around us. Before that, the Hebrews also believed the earth to be flat, and even the New Testament spoke of "the four corners of the earth." *All this is a metaphor*, the defenders of Inerrancy might now say ... but if you concede that, then why not allow that many of the emphatic, overly-conservative doctrines of today are also based on metaphor? The arrogance that caused the Church to persecute Galileo for his "heretical" cosmology, the same attitude of "I believe the Bible is inerrant and I know exactly what it means," is still underlying the thought of those who today oppose evolution and modern science.

Long after science and astronomy disproved a geocentric universe and a flat earth, there remained folks who ascribed a literal perfection to Scripture; they thus had to stubbornly force a square peg into a round hole: in this case, a rectangular earth into a spherical reality. Centuries after Galileo and Copernicus proved that the Earth is a sphere and that its rotation causes night and day, some Literalistic Christians still insisted otherwise, because their biblical approach could not allow for modern science. Even as late as the 1880s, Samuel B. Rowbotham toured England teaching that the earth is flat. Inspired by his own interpretation of Scripture, Rowbotham enthusiastically distributed his 16-page pamphlet, "Zetetic Astronomy: A Description of Several Experiments which Prove that the Surface of the Sea Is a Perfect Plane and that the Earth Is Not a Globe." He was quite emphatic. And quite wrong.

The lesson in all this seems to be that defending Inerrancy and Literalism with tunnel vision and arrogance eventually discredits Christianity. Literalism is, to state it bluntly, a lazy oversimplification. If we wish for our faith to be passed on successfully to the next generation, we must be more open-minded regarding academic and scientific progress.

Questions for Thought, Study and Group Discussion

Try the following exercise: after reading each following statement below (often asserted by various Christian denominations), add the word "but" and state an opinion that counters or qualifies the "factoid." It may be best to avoid stating your own opinion (instead, use commonly-heard qualifications that often go alongside these principles in general society) ... this is not meant to be an argumentative debate over these controversial topics ... the object of this exercise is to experience the ambiguity and paradox often found in "moral principles" (NOT to tear down or argue against the principles, but to **think**):

1. The Bible states, "Thou shalt not kill," but ...
2. The Bible states that Jesus has overcome the darkness, but ...
3. The Bible has statements against homosexual practice, but ...

If time permits delve further into the question of why homosexuality has become such a hot-button issue, when the Bible has even more rules against other things, like eating shellfish and ham, wearing gold (yes, even in the New Testament!), women with uncovered heads in church, etc. Discuss why you think many churches have kept strict prohibitions for homosexual couples who maintain fidelity — while yet relaxing other social and dietary rules?

Paradox 3

Scripture is trustworthy, but Literalism and a closed mind make it untrustworthy.

Reflective Quote for Chapter 3

Let go of certainty. The opposite isn't uncertainty. It's openness, curiosity and a willingness to embrace paradox, rather than choose up sides. The ultimate challenge is to accept ourselves exactly as we are, but never stop trying to learn and grow.

~ *Tony Schwartz, CEO of the Energy Project*

Chapter 4

The Paradox of Fear χ Fear Not (or Love v. Fear)

I must not fear. Fear is the mind-killer. Fear is the little-death that brings total obliteration. I will face my fear.
~ *Frank Herbert, through the voice of Paul Atriedes in* Dune

God is Love ... There is no fear in love. But perfect love drives out fear ...
~ *1st John 4, excerpts*

Fear, reverence and awe are normal responses when a person encounters the almighty God, Creator of the universe. Imagine an alien spaceship lands in your yard, having the technology to cross intergalactic space, and a large, armed, monstrous being steps out ... only a fool would approach it with a shotgun and a scowl! So, the Old Testament is obviously correct that "Fear is the beginning of wisdom." Most holy books do caution us to "Fear God." Nevertheless, by definition, a meaningful relationship with a Loving God **must transcend fear.**

While the Bible does speak of awestruck reverence as appropriate responses to holy encounters, more frequently we find verses telling us to "Be not afraid." In the announcement of the birth of the Christ-child, the first words from the annunciating angel's lips were: "Fear not!" Jesus himself repeatedly said, "Do not be afraid!" The First Epistle of John, Chapter 4, insists that fear and perfect love are not compatible.

Nevertheless, I grew up within a Southern religious atmosphere of **theological fear.**

Pulpit Horror Stories

At 12 years of age, I visited a friend's church for their "youth revival," where an unsmiling pastor spent thirty minutes convincing my friends and me that we were condemned to Hell. His presentation was scarier than any horror movie, because we assumed he was speaking truth. Unlike a movie, we couldn't walk out of this "theater." The traveling evangelist presented graphic details about worms crawling through our dead bodies, relentlessly-searing flames, and indescribable agony stretching out for us into eternity. Here was the preacher's first fib: he said the agony was *indescribable* ... yet he managed to spend thirty minutes describing it! Most of what the unpleasant little man told us did not come from the Bible, yet, being as it was shouted with such fierce authority, we believed it. Fear and blind belief sent us all to the altar rail for a "salvation experience."

In the weeks that followed, I could not help but notice that most of us "saved" kids were indistinguishable in our words and actions from the "unsaved" kids. I am not dismissing the value of faith in God, as I certainly *have* seen powerful changes — improvements in hearts, attitudes and actions — amongst Christians after seriously accepting an invitation to faith and love. In light of all this, my pre-teen self began to wonder: "**Is *fear* compatible with a theology of love?**" As author Robert Farrar Capon put it, "People converted by fear-mongering are people converted *from* evil, but not *to* the truth."

Freedom from Fear a Pre-Requisite to Free Will

Let's assume that a loving God offers humans Free Will. Would it be fair for God to expect us to freely search for the truths of religion within a framework of fear? For many children and youth, "having doubts" becomes associated with the fear of losing one's salvation. Doubt and fear become co-mingled. Many Christians (and many Muslims, for that matter) become fearful at the prospect of applying reasonable thought to their faith.

Various churches, pastors and denominations have warned us against "trusting" anything other than the Bible, invoking the fear that doubts, questions or any attempt to interpret Scripture beyond a surface literalism is a highway to Hell.

This book challenges you to step outside of your fear (and maybe any brainwashing from childhood) to seek a deeper understanding, an intelligent, genuine spirituality that goes beyond bumper stickers.

Courage and Encouragement

Take up the challenge to re-examine the meaning of this literal Bible verse: "The fear of the Lord is the beginning of wisdom …"[48] Proverbs conveys a Jewish emphasis, not necessarily a Christian one. The phrase "the fear of the Lord" is found 79 times in the Old Testament (Jewish scriptures), but only twice in the New Testament![49] By contrast, consider Isaiah 41:10: "So do not fear, for I am with you; do not be dismayed, for I am your God." As a whole, the Bible offers far more encouragement than any inducements to fear.

The New Testament tells us that **fear and love are not compatible**. For example, 2nd Timothy 1:7 asserts: "For God has not given us the spirit of fear; but of power, and of love, and of a sound mind." Reason and love trump fear. 1st John 4:18 echoes: "There is no fear in love. But perfect love drives out fear, because fear has to do with punishment. The one who fears is not made perfect in love."

This should settle the matter for most Christians … except for those reluctant to accept the principle that the New Testament supersedes the Old. So, let's reconsider the Old Testament use of the "fear of the Lord" phrase.

Fear or Fear Not? What the Old Testament Says

As mentioned above, an oft-quoted "fear" verse is Proverbs 1.7: "The fear of the Lord is the beginning of wisdom …" An accurate Hebrew rendering of the verse is: "Awe of Jehovah is a starting point for wisdom ..." But fear is not the end-goal of a faith journey.

Proverbs states that a "fool" never reflects on the fact that death by disaster or wild beast is nothing compared to standing before the God of all time and space, the God who controls eternity. But that is a statement about perspective, not a recommendation to live in fear. Proverbs 1:33 calls us to stand in awe of God, but then to move forward to a life "without fear of harm."

Indeed, the Hebrew word rendered "fear" in English — in the context of encountering God — is a complex mix of being intimidated by the Almighty Mystery, yet also an emotion of **joy**. As the venerated *Interpreter's Dictionary of the Bible* puts it, biblical *fear of God* is "not merely negative. It accompanies the perception of God's glory and may generate an emotion of exultation and joy at the discovery of God's intense concern and love" for us.[50] Thus "fear of God" is another paradox, because it is often mixed with a joyful trust in the power of the Divine Majesty, such as in the Psalms, ("Serve ye Jehovah with fear, And rejoice with trembling."[51]), and Matthew 28:8 ("... afraid yet filled with joy ..."). In both Old and New Testaments, the end result of "fearing the Lord" is to have a sense of sacred awe, reverence, and respect for God, coupled with joy and hope in divine, saving love.

New Testament Approach to the "Fear of God"

In the Old Testament, the positive emotions that accompanied an encounter with an awe-inspiring God were more of a *future* hope. The New Testament (New Covenant) makes the positive side of fear more explicit and immediate. Early in Luke's gospel, we find the unsettling appearance of angels begins with fear but quickly turns to joy. When Zechariah saw an angel, he was "startled and gripped with fear," but the angel said "Do not be afraid ...", and then spoke of a coming "joy and delight" and "good news."[52] Next, shepherds "were terrified" until the angel said to them, "Do not be afraid. I bring you good news that will cause great joy for all the people."[53]

The "fear of the Lord" phrase, used so frequently in the Old Testament, only appears twice in the New: Acts 9:31 speaks of "walking in the fear of the Lord," but this verse is translated in several respected Bible versions as "reverence," not fear. The Message (MSG) version gets it right by replacing "fear" with "a deep sense of reverence for God."

The only other place we find this "fear of the Lord" phrase within the New Testament is in Paul's Second Letter to the Corinthians. Here the Hebrew word is actually even stronger than a mere cautious fear, but literally a "terror."[54] But is Paul suggesting we live that way, that terror should be the hallmark of our faith understanding? No! The greater context here is the promise of heaven. Paul first speaks of facing death and judgment, and how the thought of that — including the realization that we are mortal and powerless before God — can induce terror. But that is only a momentary Pauline consideration. In contrast to the word "terror," look at the words Paul uses in the same passage to describe the "good news": *life, eternal home, guarantee, confidence.* He concluded the section by joyfully proclaiming, "So from now on we regard no one from a worldly point of view ... [For] if anyone is in Christ, that person is new creation." The old, worldly view (the common view of Paul's day) was of trembling before a terrible god who could, like Zeus, bring thunderbolts of death and judgment. But the New Way, Paul concludes, is of the path of love and reconciliation; in the Christian era, God "does not count people's sins against them."[55]

A Healthy View of Fear

Sometimes fear is healthy. It would be a horrible parent who failed to teach their toddler to fear sticking a fork into an electrical outlet. As a six-year-old visiting my grandmother's home near a swamp, I encountered a coiled snake. Instantly struck with fear, I backed away and ran to safety. Obviously, fear can be a good thing!

But most forms of fear are just plain **evil**. Living daily in a state of fear is the opposite of Goodness. The worst tyrants and dictators of history used fear to control the masses. Each day in our world, in various homes and businesses, tiny "dictators" use fear to control their spouse or their employee with threats. Anytime fear is induced, pain/anxiety is the result. Stress is both physically and emotionally unhealthy. Fear robs folks of their freedom — and enslavement is synonymous with sheer evil.

Is it possible that some preachers perpetrate evil when they frighten children? The evangelists intend to "save souls," and simplistically assume they can count all those bowing and trembling at the altar as wonderful achievements for God. But I have observed that many of those who only came to a "relationship" with God via intimidation, whose ensuing faith is rooted in fear, frequently drift away from religion later in life.

Yes, some converts eventually move beyond their initial fear-induced salvation to discover the deeper truths of a Loving God. But would they have eventually come to God anyway? Would God abandon people only because they never stumbled into a revival tent and heard a hellfire-and-brimstone sermon? I once overheard a wise old pastor tell why he didn't preach such angry, pulpit-thumping sermons: "Why would I try to scare people into heaven, when God Himself never uses that tactic?"

If fear was a legitimate means for bringing people into a faith relationship, God would routinely appear in the sky with a flaming sword and scream, "Bow to me or else!" Since God does not do this, but instead allows us to have Free Will, we should reject fear as a tool of manipulation.

False Answers to Real Fear

In this life, things *do* go bump in the night, and in the day ... people face palpable, everyday fears. Ironically, Fundamentalists offer an answer to the real fears of life by not taking suffering seriously enough. The flippant answers some "prosperity" pastors offer up (such as, "If you just have enough faith!") are not only cruel to those who suffer, but may drive away the intelligent person of faith. A friend of mine, and a believer, told me this account of the fakery that can accompany "positive-thinking," God-can-heal-all evangelists. He accompanied another friend, who was a quadriplegic, to a glamorous spectacle of a healing service. The preacher had the praise band play redundant, trance inducing music over and over as the crowd swayed and sang and marched around the meeting hall. The self-described faith-healer descended from the pulpit mount, down into the crowd, laying his hands on people, "healing" them of minor ailments and "slaying" them in the spirit, casting out their demons, etc.

My friend said he watched as the preacher poured his confidence and charisma onto people with unseen diseases, bad backs, migraines and such ... and then stopped dead in his tracks when he spied our friend in the wheelchair. This was not an ordinary wheelchair, but an elaborate device to hold her in place (as she had no control or movement from her neck down) and which carried a breathing respirator. She was so thoroughly paralyzed that even her lungs would not work without assistance. My friend said that as soon the preacher glimpsed all this, he abruptly spun around and returned to the pulpit. This "healer," who preached so confidently about how faith can heal anything, knew the odds were that he would not be effective with a quadriplegic. His "power of suggestion healing" or the placebo effect had a near-zero chance of raising the immobilized patient from her wheelchair.

Incidentally, I do believe in healing and miracles. I've seen and heard some amazing things. But I have never seen, in my 60 years, a severed spinal cord re-generated by faith. Perhaps you have, but it is rare.

A Real Miracle: A Faith that Faces Tragedy

On a Palm Sunday in 1994, Goshen United Methodist Church had a full house of Christians praising God with the jubilation usually present on the Sunday before Easter. Then, without warning, a monster tornado struck, reducing the church to rubble, killing twenty congregants and injuring over ninety. The minister's own precious little daughter, Hannah Clem, was one of those killed. Tragic. And theologically challenging.

Could God not have nudged the tornado a few feet aside and saved the worshippers on that Holy Palm Sunday? Or made it an F2 instead of an F4? Or delayed the tornado an hour, and let Hannah Clem live? These are not questions which TV prosperity-preachers wish to hear; celeb-pastor Joel Osteen does not want anything dimming his blinding-white smile and positive prattle.

Through an amazing exercise of faith, the Reverend Kelly Clem buried her daughter, and then she led the survivors of the Palm Sunday tragedy as they re-convened to praise the Risen Christ on Easter Sunday. She did not throw out some cheap or easy clichés to her congregation, she did not casually say "This is God's plan" or "All things work together for the good." After all, she was grieving her own innocent child. Pastor Clem had a solid, thoughtful, mature theology and faith. She did not try to explain away the mysteries of God by using trite, one-dimensional answers. She had the amazingly strong faith to say genuinely that she still trusted God — because she had a sense of the eternal, a faith perspective, not a "scientific answer."

Another Faith-Testing Tornado

A friend of mine had given over one hundred thousand dollars of his own money and years of his time to build and run a Christian airplane ministry. His work was purely altruistic, helping fly needy cancer victims to treatment centers without charge. When donations would not fully cover their costs, he had no choice but to skip paying property insurance. A tornado struck the airplane hangar, destroying it and the planes inside, bringing the ministry to a halt. My friend said, with good humor (mimicking Ricky Ricardo) but also with real pathos, "God's got some 'splainin' to do!" Forgive me for citing these tragedies, I do not intend to make light of them nor reduce such monumental events to mere "object lessons." But they do force us to face the hard question: If God is good, why does God allow such mindless calamity?

If God were truly micro-managing human life, one would think there'd be no deaths of preachers' innocent children, or the destruction of fine churches and important ministries with tornadoes. Yet I heard some Christians say that Hurricane Katrina, which hit New Orleans with a fury, was God's punishment against Sin City. They fail to explain why the area of New Orleans with the *least* damage was Bourbon Street and the French Quarter. The booze bars and strip joints were back up and running in short order. Perhaps God is not a micro-manager after all.

Fear and Tragedy Are Real, but So Are Love and Trust

The answer to evil, fear and tragedy is too big for this particular book. The problem of theodicy, of why God allows evil, has been addressed better by authors like C. S. Lewis, Phillip Yancey and Rabbi Harold Kushner, to name a few. As a pastor, I never tossed my parishioners a simple pat answer, because even if a cliché gives them peace for today, they wake up tomorrow twice as troubled.

There is no single, easy answer to theodicy, but possibilities include:

God allowed us Free Will and has placed a certain amount of randomness into creation as a necessary part of God's Grander Plan.

God is infinite, we are finite, and cannot understand all mysteries. This is not heaven.

We have a dark, "Good Friday" view of things, but one day we shall have an Easter (resurrected) view ... it is certainly within the powers of an omnipotent God to make all things right at some future time.

But don't tell me it is right *today*. Don't tickle my theological taste buds with Pollyanna aphorisms that turn out to be like cotton candy: empty of nutritional substance, spineless and thoughtless and collapsing in even a gentle rain. We should not be fooled by snake-oil salesmen. We should not let fear drive our beliefs; we should not be afraid to hear Truth; we should courageously face reality.

In the Quantum Age

In an increasingly scientific age, we Christians should quit trying to explain everything and inserting a dubious "Creation science" into faith, because faith is, first of all, about the spiritual and the mysterious. And we should stop drawing our circles of inclusion and doctrine so small and tight that more people are outside than in. Otherwise, **Christianity will continue to lose reasonable people to skepticism because we are making unreasonable claims**.

Ironically, what this cynical, scientific age is longing for is a little bit of mystery. It's okay to say, "A large part of God is an infinite, unseen Spirit, therefore we acknowledge the divine mystery." The Universe is beyond our imaginations in its scope. So, don't be uncomfortable with the concept of an infinite, mysterious God. God *is* supernatural ... but we cannot bottle the supernatural into magic elixirs or lucky charms. We believe in eternal life. But we also recognize that this present life is filled with questions and suffering ... and our faith cannot make that hard reality disappear.

Questions for Thought, Study and Group Discussion

Read the First Letter of John, Chapter 4. Key concepts include "God is love," and "Perfect love drives out fear." Discuss how these may seem like a paradox, or an outright contradiction, of the Old Testament idea of God as wrathful, and of verses like "Fear of God is the beginning of wisdom."

If you are willing: Share/discuss your childhood experiences with God and Church. How much was fear or awe involved vs. peace and joy? (Next question is related.)

Again, thinking back to your childhood but also currently: Has the threat of Hell been a positive or negative in your life? Note: A full discussion of how you imagine the Afterlife to be is not really the aim here. Here the discussion should center on the topic of Fear and Trust of God. See Chapter 8 for more on the topic of Hell.

Paradox 4

Fear of God is called the beginning of Wisdom, but God's Love drives out fear.

Reflective Quote for Chapter 4

In God I trust; I will not be afraid. What can mere mortals do to me?

~ *Psalm 56:4*

Chapter 5

The Paradox of an Eternal God χ Changeable God

If you don't like change, you're going to like irrelevance even less.
~ *General Eric Shinseki, Chief of Staff, US Army*

No man ever steps in the same river twice.
~ *Heraclitus*

Conservatives and Traditionalists have a worthy position: we should respect and follow the principles and virtues that have been **successfully proven** across centuries of life experience. Progressives also have a worthy proposition: as scientific knowledge expands, as societies become more complex and less homogenous, and as cultures evolve, we do well to **foster flexibility and tolerance**. Many of our society's religious controversies — and much squabbling within denominations — are rooted in this clash between those who are willing to adapt to a changing world versus those who adhere to established standards. Theologically, these two groups (Progressives vs. Conservatives) view God and Scripture in diametrically different ways. Progressives emphasize the need to consider Scripture's context and metaphorical meaning, and that flexibility extends to a less-circumscribed view of God as changeable or adaptive to the times. Conservatives pledge allegiance to a literal reading of Hebrews 13:9: "God is the same yesterday and today and forever." Near-opposite approaches, yet within my Paradox Paradigm, both have value.

Bound to Change

From a numerical standpoint, Religious Conservatives seem to be winning the debate. Conservative churches that preach literalism and stasis are growing, and "liberal" denominations are in decline. I predict, however, that the statistical success of Conservative Fundamentalism is bound to fall. Why? Because betting against *change* would be like betting against tomorrow's sunrise. Yes, that's a paradoxical metaphor: the reality of *change* is as sure as sunrise. Human history and cosmic history both demonstrate the inevitability and ubiquity of flux and variation. Put simply, **change is always and everywhere**. Even things which seem ancient and constant, like the Milky Way galaxy, for example, are in ever-spiraling movement and flux.

Raised as a devout Christian, philosopher Alfred North Whitehead began to re-assess metaphysics as he was exposed to the emerging "modern" science of the early twentieth century. By 1929, having rejected creedal religion, he asserted that *change* is an inescapable, fundamental feature of reality; he emphasized that "all things flow." He was not attacking spiritual belief, but he raised concerns and doubts about the dogmatism of organized religion, even while attacking scientific materialism as "the fallacy of misplaced concreteness."[56] In other words, his observation of widespread **change** caused him to question orthodoxy in both fields: religion *and* science. But even Whitehead could not have imagined the drastic changes in science, technology and society since then.

Long before Whitehead, the Greek philosopher Heraclitus (see this chapter's heading quote, above) also insisted that **ever-present change is a fundamental trait of the universe**. Although born five centuries before Jesus, Heraclitus used the same word as John's gospel — *Logos* — to describe the divine, active, unifying force of logic permeating the universe. Some accused Heraclitus of being an agnostic or atheist, yet he embraced the concept of a god — in fact, a monotheistic God consistent with

Christianity. He certainly thought in ways that would later be part of Christian/Johannine theology. Heraclitus appeals to me because he also emphasized the key role of paradox. The *Logos*, Heraclitus taught, brings a "hidden harmony" out of Paradox by binding "opposites together in a unified tension, which is like that of a lyre, where a stable harmonious sound emerges from the tension of the opposing forces [of] the string."

In the debate between Change vs. Constancy, Change wins hands down — everywhere outside of religious fundamentalism, that is. The Humanities and the Sciences agree with Heraclitus, that the river of reality is never the same.

But does the opinion of "pagans" matter to people of faith?

Plundering the Egyptians ... and the Greeks

The phrase, "Plundering the Egyptians," taken from the Book of Exodus, was used by St. Augustine of Hippo (and others) to bless the practice of gleaning the best from pagan wisdom. In other words, Moses didn't just take the Egyptians' silver and gold, but also "borrowed" aspects of their culture and science. So, Bishop Augustine argued that Scripture defends the use of "pagan wisdom," including knowledge gleaned from Greek philosophers and scientists, beginning with Plato. Instead of arguing that Truth is a monopoly owned solely by Christians, Augustine proposed that we "borrow" truth/knowledge wherever we find it, purifying it of any false dross. **"All truth is God's truth,"** Augustine famously stated.

Modern Conservative Christians may cringe at the idea of gaining insights from such "pagan" philosophers. Founders of Christianity did not have that fear. Early Church Father Justin Martyr wrote in his second-century tome, *First Apology* (as in, "Christian apologetics"), that both Socrates and Heraclitus were "Christians before Christ." Justin Martyr was certainly as committed to the faith — and to the authority of Scripture — as any modern-day "biblical conservative," ultimately proving it via martyrdom. Given the option to denounce his Christian faith and escape a horrible death at the hands of Roman persecutors, he instead answered, "No one who is rightly minded turns from true belief to false." Nevertheless, Justin was open-minded, having previously asserted that "those who lived reasonably are Christians, even though they have been thought atheists; as, among the Greeks, Socrates and Heraclitus ..." And there is another interesting connection with Justin and Heraclitus: as *Wikipedia* puts it, he "is regarded as the foremost interpreter of the theory of the Logos ..." Justin believed that science and philosophy add to our understanding of God.

Justin Martyr was far from alone in being happy to learn from other, even pagan, philosophers. I could cite more. But now, as we continue to prove the case that church history does **not** show a monolithic or inflexible view when it comes to Literalism vs. Scientific thinking, let's move into yet another controversial area: Evolution.

Is Evolution God's Tool?

When I was young, Darwinian Evolution began to be taught in my public school. Yes, even in Alabama. My older brother had a keen interest in, and knowledge of, science. My father was a minister schooled in the late 1930s at a conservative seminary. Yet both my brother and father told me the same thing: "You can be a Christian and still believe that Evolution is a reasonable theory ... God uses Evolution as one of His tools of Creation." There was no inconsistency, in our minds.

Now we know that there are some problems with Darwin's theory of genetic adaption. He did not have the advantage of modern technologies, and certainly had no grasp of molecular biology — much less quantum biology. Natural selection does not explain all the complexities of biological reproduction and the adaptation/evolution of species. The cutting edge of research does, indeed, involve quantum mechanics (see Chapter 11 for more on quantum biology). Nevertheless, the core of Darwin's idea — that "nature" has processes for adaptation to environment and systems for the progressive advancement of organisms — still remains true. What has this to do with religion? Three things:

1. Acceptance of the principle of Evolution does not rule out believing in God as our Creator.
2. All the evidence points to a progressive evolution of living organisms, and not a "steady-state." Therefore, it seems that the characteristic of growth and changeability is part of God's nature. Change and growth are God's *modus operandi*.
3. Early church writers had no problem understanding the Genesis creation story as a metaphor, not as a detailed, fact-oriented science lesson. It was only later that biblical conservatives insisted upon a word-for-word non-symbolical approach to Genesis. As I promised, let me cite a few examples, below.

Clement of Alexandria did not believe that the seven days of Creation were actual 24-hour days. A devout Christian, he nevertheless had no problem being in dialogue with the "pagan" wisdom of Egypt and Greece in his quest to understand the deeper symbolism of Genesis.[57]

Irenaeus, Bishop of Lyons: In the second century, this bishop was a key figure in confronting heresy, and defending — and defining — Orthodoxy. Yet he believed the Genesis creation story should be taken **allegorically** (i.e. interpreting a particular Scripture not as a history lesson but as a metaphorical moral or spiritual lesson).[58]

Origen of Alexandria, (c. 184–253 CE), explicitly opposed those who interpreted the Creation Story as an historical or scientific account of how God created the world. There were other voices before Origen who also advocated symbolic interpretations of the creation story, but Origen was one of the most influential in establishing early church thought on the issue. Origen stressed that Scripture was divinely inspired, but he outlined three different ways ("body, soul and spirit") in which Scripture passages can be interpreted. He taught that the first two chapters of Genesis (the creation stories) had no literal meaning at all and must be understood allegorically.[59] Origen wrote this regarding the Genesis creation story: "I do not suppose that anyone doubts that these things figuratively indicate certain mysteries, the history having taken place in appearance, and not literally."[60]

Even the Bible itself, referring to events in Genesis, quotes **Paul** as having said that these "things are an allegory ..."[61]

To be fair, many others in Early Christendom did argue that Genesis should be taken as literal history. But the literal dogmatism of "Creation Science" and "Young Creationism," which ridiculously asserts that believing otherwise "destroys confidence in Scripture," is a more recent stance.

Considering myself grounded in the wisdom of the early church mothers and fathers — many of them martyrs and true saints — means I don't shrink under the shrill criticism by contemporary, rightwing "saints" against my understanding of God's Word as symbolical and metaphorical. I am not alone.

The Paradox of a Changeable yet Steadfast God

That was a long digression to arrive at this assertion: the dogmatic claim for an instant Creation or a steady-state, unchanging nature of God's cosmos is not supported by science, church history, or Scripture. Heraclitus was right about "Change" being an inescapable part of the universe. Thus, my thesis is that **God and God's Creation is more about change than about constancy**. The paradox here is that God is "steadfast," (as the Bible states), yet **God's manner of relating to humans has changed**. God is

Eternally Steadfast yet Ever-moving.

This is an important debate. It affects modern society in myriad ways, most recently and most controversially in the debate over feminism and sexuality. How do conservative Christian and Muslim sects move forward in our Western Civilization that has largely adopted equality for women, and a "live and let live" approach toward homosexuals? The Old Testament (and the Qur'an) treats women as second-class citizens, and prohibits homosexual practice as "an abomination." Yet later in time, the New Testament asserts that "in Christ Jesus you are all children of God ... there is neither Jew nor Gentile ... nor is there male and female, for you are all one in Christ Jesus" (Galatians 3:26–28, excerpted, but true to context).

I've heard many debates between "liberal" and "conservative" Christians, each side quoting various verses to defend an "anti-homosexual" stance vs. an "accepting" approach. From a purely-logical standpoint (as if I were judging competing College Debate Teams), both sides have valid points. I don't have the solution to the quandary in Christendom on this issue ... except to ask: "Why not err on the side of love?" My conservative friends say, "We cannot ignore Scripture!" To which I answer: I cannot abandon the core teachings of Christ (Love, Grace, and Non-Judgmental Acceptance) for the sake of clinging to Scriptural literalism.

As important as the sexuality issue is, there are additional issues of importance here. We must move forward in ways to keep ancient faiths valid for our time — **without eroding the authority of Scripture.**

The Way Forward

Yes, I'm asserting that God changes the human-divine relationship, even while I am well aware of this verse: "For I the Lord do not change" (Malachi 3:6). Here again, we must not be lazy; we must look at the context. That third chapter begins with a reference to the coming New Covenant (which would be a huge change), and ends with God speaking of compassion. Malachi's message is that the core character of God (love and forgiveness) will not change. But Malachi is the last book of the Old Testament, and in that very book and chapter, God is announcing an upcoming change in the special connection with the "His children."[62]

After considering the verses that, according to some, claim God never changes, we must balance them with these verses: from Exodus 32:14: "So the LORD changed His mind ...", and in Amos 7:3: "The Lord changed His mind about this." Look at the context and full meaning of these verses, and guess what you'll discover? God changed/reversed the earlier decisions!

In the New Testament, Jesus at first refused to help a Canaanite woman, saying, "I was sent only to the lost sheep of Israel." But she persuades him to change his mind, and then he granted her request.[63] To my ear, this was a somewhat playful or humorous exchange meant to teach a lesson to his disciples (who had asked Jesus to "send her away"). But for a Bible literalist to be consistent, they would have to view this as another verse in which God's mind **changed**.

Even if you are not comfortable saying that God can "evolve," human society does indeed evolve and change. So organized religion must adapt ... or die. God *is* changeable when it comes to relationships. The God of the Bible factored in different approaches according to the cultures of the times. Ecclesiastes states: "God has made everything suitable for its time; moreover, he has put a sense of past and future into their minds, yet [mortals] cannot find out what God has done from the beginning to the end."[64] The way for the Church to move beyond a fossilized, two-thousand-year-old orthodoxy is to understand that **God has more flexibility than we do.**

The Word "New" in *New Testament*
Indeed, it seems odd to view God as unchangeable, when

the New Covenant — the New Testament — is predicated on something NEW! We know that God's way of relating to New Testament Christians was a sea change from the Old Testament rigidity. And we've already shown that God was portrayed as changeable in the Old Testament. Yet another verse: in Exodus 32:9–14, Moses pleads with God to change His plan to destroy the Israelites, and verse 14 states, "the Lord relented ..."

If God can change "His" own mind, God can also choose to change the way He relates to humanity over time. I've purposely used the patriarchal language of the Old Testament — *God = He* — to raise yet another example. There is value and validity in the modern movement to change our "male-dominated" language. (Usually, I employ inclusive language in all my books.) Does the Bible ever say we must speak of God exclusively with "male" metaphors? No. In fact, Jesus referred to himself as a "mother hen." The Old Testament speaks of God with the metaphor of Divine Wisdom, which in the Greek *Septuagint*, is the very feminine word, *Sophia* ("wisdom/sophistry"). To a rather-primitive civilization that depended on the "animal strength" of male hunter-warrior-leaders, it is not surprising that God portrayed "Himself" as a Father. But again, the later revelation of God in Christ embraces the "feminine" side of humanity: Jesus openly wept, emphasized the importance of nurturing children and tenderly took them to his lap, washed his disciples' feet like a maidservant, spoke of himself as a "mother hen," and portrayed God as a female in his parables (see Luke 13:34 and 15:8–10).

This is not radical feminism; this is biblical common sense. To be clear, I don't see anything wrong with calling God "Father" ("Abba"). Jesus — a man, after all — will always remain a "He" in my mind. And even feminist professor Virginia Ramey Mollenkott admits that "Neuter language is very impersonal," and that "warmly relational metaphors of God as Father, Mother, Friend, or Comforter" have their place.[65] Nevertheless, the post-modern change of language toward inclusiveness is a good change. The infinite, quantum God most certainly is way bigger than *any* metaphor regarding gender. And it seems to me that the New Testament does intend to change our perception of God beyond a purely male gender, toward the ideal unity of Galatians 3: "In Christ ... there is no male or female."

Red Letter Radical

Yes, the proof of this "changeable God" is most clearly seen in the New Covenant, and in the very words of Jesus (often printed in red letters in modern Bibles). As mentioned earlier, Jesus said he came not to abolish the law but to fulfill it. *Fulfillment* means accomplishing or completing; according to orthodoxy, once Salvation by Grace was achieved through Christ's actions via the Cross and the Resurrection, the Law was "fulfilled" (Matthew 5:17). The New Covenant, the new order of things, began. Nothing indicates *change and adaptation* more than the word, "new," and as it happens, the word "new" is used extensively throughout the New Testament.

Jesus overtly contradicted or re-directed Jewish Law. In a previous chapter, we examined the fact that Jesus reversed the Old Testament Law regarding retribution. Jesus said in Matthew 5:38–39: "You have heard that it was said, 'Eye for eye, and tooth for tooth.' But I tell you, do not resist an evil person ..." Jesus is almost calling the Old Testament *hearsay* ("You have heard it said ..."). Then with "turn the other cheek," he then unambiguously disagrees with, and radically changes, the Torah Law!

Ninety-eight percent of Christians understand that the requirements of God's Old Testament Law have changed, particularly regarding social norms and rules of diet and cleanliness.[66] Even the most conservative Christians admit that "New Testament Christians" are no longer required to follow all the kosher Jewish laws. Jesus began this change by intentionally failing to wash his hands (see Luke 11:37–4). He also violated (intentionally, it seems) Sabbath rules, and ignored prohibitions against touching the "unclean."

The Christian sea change regarding Jewish law was clarified and expanded in the Book of Acts. A fresh revelation, given to Peter in the Book of Acts, allowed the expanding Gentile Church to be free of Hebrew worries regarding diet. Then Paul changed the Old Testament Law regarding circumcision. In this regard, Jesus, Peter and Paul did not model the strict, inflexible slavishness to Scripture that most Conservative Fundamentalists are comfortable with nowadays. I hope these points help those with a Christian viewpoint to consider[67] that God's standards can be changeable. Perhaps the best way to word it is that the way God applies religious precepts in *relation* to human behavior has changed, and thus is changeable.

Religious Evolution

So, we do see a progression from the earliest Old Testament books to a more sophisticated, grace-based New Testament understanding of God's plan. You can argue that "God never changes," but **God's rules and laws most certainly did change**. Look at what Peter reported in Acts 10:9–15. Peter had a vision in which God spoke to him. It forever changed Christianity. God told Peter to eat animals that had previously been forbidden by the Bible (the Torah), because they were "unclean." Now a new Law came. "The Lord" stated three times to Peter, "Do not call anything impure that God has made clean." Contrast those words from the Lord (via Peter) in Acts of the New Testament to the Old Testament Laws of Leviticus. For example, Leviticus 11:42–44 quotes God's emphatic command: "You are not to eat any creature that moves along the ground, whether it moves on its belly or walks on all fours or on many feet; it is unclean. Do not defile yourselves by any of these creatures. Do not make yourselves unclean by means of them ... consecrate yourselves and be holy, because I am holy." There is no question the Law shifted 180 degrees from Old Testament to New. God's rules changed, maybe because the *people* to whom God spoke *did change*.

I am not ignorant of the biblical statement, "Jesus Christ is the same yesterday and today and forever" (Hebrews 13:8). But I am challenging those who read too much into that statement. The true nature of God is trustworthy, and we can count on God's love and mercy today and forever. But there is no doubt the Bible shows God's flexibility and willingness to adapt regarding Christ's manner of relating to us. We see that Scriptural interpretation and application changed over time — Jesus himself was very "Liberal" in putting new twists to old Scriptures.

1st Peter 1:23–25 speaks of "the living and enduring word of God" as something that "endures forever." The word of God can refer both/either to Jesus (called the *Logos* or *Word* in several Scriptures) and to the Bible. Jesus was a living, breathing, growing individual … he changed from being a baby in a manger, to an inquisitive 12-year-old in the Temple, to a grown man. Thus, a "flexible Word," if you will. And as for the Bible as an "unchanging Word," the writers of the Bible never saw or knew what the final, canonized Scripture would become. I take from this another paradox: the Scripture "Word" and the Living "Word" (Christ) are both eternal and steadfast, yet not fossilized or static … not set in stone, but forever alive in Spirit.

A Postscript on Time and Infinity

When considering a "Quantum God," we should add to this chapter a few thoughts about God and Time from the scientific perspective. Here again we find a Paradox. Quantum Theory (including Einstein's Theory of Relativity) views Time as **both** constant and changeable.

Constant: Time is constant, for all practical purposes, on our planet. For example, the unstable isotope Uranium 238 decomposes until it becomes a stable element (Lead), and the time this takes is a fixed 6.5 billion years from start to finish. As radioactive Uranium decays, it passes through various stages, becoming various isotopes for predictable lengths of time. When Uranium becomes Polonium 214, that step only lasts 0.00016 of a second within the 6.5 billion-year process. As best as scientists can tell, the "clock" on this hasn't changed. Thus, it's no surprise that the International Standard for the length of one second is based on radioactive decay. This is how atomic clocks have a near-perfect precision, losing only one second in 100 million years.[68]

Changeable: But in the quantum view, Time *is* flexible. Quantum theorists (including Einstein) point to the fact that Time can bend or even stop within a Black Hole. The theorists also speak of a speed-induced dilation of time, such as the so-called "twins paradox," where one twin brother takes a journey in a near-light-speed spaceship, then returns to earth without aging, but finds that his stay-at-home twin is gray-haired and feeble.[69] Einstein himself stated, "People like us, who believe in [quantum] physics, know that **the distinction between past, present, and future is only a stubbornly persistent illusion.**"

All that validates my thesis: in a quantum and cosmic sense, God can be "the same yesterday, today and forever" AND, paradoxically, God can be in flux. At a basic, material level, God is stable and consistent *vis-à-vis* humanity. Simultaneously (ironically, "simultaneously" is a word about *timing*), God stands above Time and Space. God is infinite, eternal and immune to the constraints we finite-thinking creatures try to impose. In other words, the whole debate about an unchangeable God may well be an irrelevant human construct.

Summary of Summaries ... So Far

This book does not attempt a thorough debate between Science and Faith or Evolution and Religion — an argument that seems ultimately irrelevant to my faith. Rather, the aim here is to drive home the radical notion that **orthodoxy *must* change**. We are losing educated young people when we trot out tired old positions of anti-science.

It may help the reader if we now summarize earlier points and look ahead to points yet to come:

1. We must apply our God-given brains to properly understand Scripture, to understand the complexity of its context, and to know which scriptures are most applicable to our place and time as post-modern, New Testament Christians.

2. God is eternal and reliable "yesterday, today and tomorrow," but we are not: we change. As human civilization changes, our ability to understand and apply God's Word changes.

3. God gave us, and gives us, ever greater revelation and understanding of the Word. Many of the harsh rules which applied to the savage, nomadic tribe of early Jews are no longer demanded of us under the New Covenant.

Even those who say "we must take the Bible literally" don't actually do so. For example, consider Leviticus 20:27: "A man or woman who is a medium or spiritist among you must be put to death. You are to stone them ..." There are palm-readers in most every town, but I don't see fundamentalist Christians trying to stone them to death. Or how many Christian women have gold rings on their fingers or other adornment, seemingly in direct opposition to the command of 1st Timothy 2:9: "I also want women to dress modestly, with decency and propriety, not with braided hair or gold or pearls ..." For years, several church denominations prohibited the wearing of even a wedding band made of gold, and I know of some who would slip if off at church but wear it during the week ... humorously ironic, since the temporary removal of a wedding ring is something also practiced by promiscuous playboys.

It is not "evil" or "liberal" to admit we live in a modern, scientific culture. If we fail to equip and adapt our religion to be relevant, pragmatic and accepting in the eyes of a new generation, we would be in violation of the Great Commission, Christ's mandate to reach out, attract and teach new disciples. The Apostle Paul did not hesitate to go into the "pagan" marketplace to reach converts, even walking amidst the "false gods and idols" of Mars Hill, and using the pagan vernacular to accommodate Greek culture in order to be relevant. We can do no less.

Questions for Thought, Study and Group Discussion
Do you believe our Eternal God changes, or just that God's relationship with humans is all that changes?

Nowadays, few Jews adhere strictly to kosher dietary rules. Do you believe this is a result of: a) a theological change, a less literal reading of Levitical laws, perhaps subtly influenced by the Christian approach to such issues; b) a general decline in religiosity; c) the advent of refrigeration and other technologies that make food safer (pork and seafood, for example);

d) Or something else, or a combination of all of the above?

Do you believe our gender differences will continue after death, when we move to the next dimension (Heaven)?

Paradox 5
God is "the same yesterday, today and forever," and simultaneously, an omniscient and ever-moving God *can* change.

Reflective Quote for Chapter 5
How wonderful that we have met with a paradox. Now we have some hope of making progress.
~ Niels Bohr, pioneer of Quantum Physics

Chapter 6

The Paradox of Purpose χ Pointlessness

All is vanity ... There is no remembrance of former things; neither shall there be any remembrance of things that are to come ...
~ *Ecclesiastes 1:2,11, KJV*

Whatever you do will be insignificant, but it is very important that you do it.
~ *Mahatma Mohandas Gandhi, almost as famous as a Beatle*

All things must pass.
~ *George Harrison, a Beatle*

Whether rich and powerful, like King Solomon, or worshipped as a prophet like Gandhi, and even an idolized pop star like Beatle George Harrison, wise folks realize that nothing lasts. Today's significance becomes tomorrow's footnote. Yet, here is another paradox, (restating Gandhi's quote, above): **Your life has purpose even though your life's achievements will become meaningless.**

All Things Must Pass

Face the fact: All things will die, rust or crumble into dust. (I speak here of material *things*, not spiritual essence.) We waste energy and resources maintaining an illusion of permanence. The wealthy donate hefty sums to have their name emblazoned on a building ... a college, a hospital, a church, whatever. But even if your name is chiseled in stone, a century from now no one will know or care. Ordinary people *do* have their names in stone: on cemetery headstones. Walk through an old cemetery ... is there a single name that stands out, that has any significance to your life today? Sure, we remember the names of US Presidents from 200 years ago ... but do we actually know more than a paragraph of their biography? We certainly don't know them truly as persons; we no longer have access to their essential personality.

Ecclesiastes records the cynical ramblings of a religious leader or king (tradition ascribes it to King Solomon) who questioned his own purpose in life. The king in Ecclesiastes seems to have "had it all" ... all the lusts of this world fulfilled: wealth, power, women, food and drink, all without limit. Strikingly, he confesses complete dissatisfaction with life and is most remembered for this quote: "All is vanity."

All Things Great and Small

Many of the so-called *great* persons of history died while clinging to their delusions of grandeur and earthly immortality. Alexander the Great conquered all contenders and established one of the largest empires of the ancient world by the age of thirty. He ascribed to himself the title of "Great." He had everything: wealth, power, status. And yet, his life was cut short at a young 32, either by alcoholism or poisoning.

According to legend, on one occasion when Alexander the Great was being even more obnoxious and arrogant than usual, his wisest advisor, Diogenes, tried to teach a lesson in humility. Diogenes waited in the castle's dungeon, which also served as a mausoleum. Eventually, when Alexander wondered where his wise advisor had gone, the king was directed to the dungeon, where he found Diogenes hunched over, studying a pile of bones.

"What are you doing?" the all-powerful ruler asked.

"I am searching for the royal bones of your father," the philosopher answered, "... but I cannot seem to distinguish *his* bones from those of his slaves!"

Death conquers all.

Ozymandias *Who?*

Percy Bysshe Shelly's poem, "Ozymandias," speaks to this fleeting, illusory nature of "greatness," with a reminder that most ego-shrines don't last much longer than our flesh:

> Two vast and trunkless legs of stone
> Stand in the desert. Near them, on the sand,
> Half sunk, a shattered visage lies, whose frown,
> And wrinkled lip, and sneer of cold command,
> Tell that its sculptor well those passions read ...
> And on the pedestal these words appear:
> "My name is Ozymandias, king of kings:
> Look on my works, ye mighty, and despair!"
> [But] Nothing beside remains. Round the decay
> Of that colossal wreck, boundless and bare
> The lone and level sands stretch far away ...

Ozymandias (thought by some to be Pharaoh Ramses II) believed that by building a giant stone shrine to himself, he could cheat death and preserve an eternal legacy greater than any other. He exalted himself, dubbing himself the "king of kings." Instead, his decaying monument became a tribute to impermanence. Ozymandias has been swept into the dustbin of history ... save a poem that satirizes his foolish vanity. Despite rumors to the contrary, the King of Rock 'n Roll (Elvis) is dead, and so is the King of Pop (Michael Jackson). Kings die. Or as others have put it, at the end of the game, the kings, queens and pawns of the chess set are all tossed into the same box.

Meaninglessness ... and Hope

Meaningless vanity. Life can seem that way at times. But in the end, Solomon confessed that God indeed has a purpose. The *Amplified Bible* adds this clarification of the king's words in Ecclesiastes 3:11: God has "planted eternity in men's heart and mind (a divinely implanted sense of a purpose working through the ages)."

So even in the face of despair, we still suspect, or have hope, that God has a purpose for us. We just aren't sure what it is. As a neurotic child, my favorite way of getting out of trouble when I did something wrong was to say "I didn't do it on purpose." This could be a sad epitaph for all too many people. I would not want those words engraved on my tombstone: "I didn't do life on purpose." Why go through life aimlessly, living only for self, without purpose or direction?

Most humans search for meaning. An Oxford-based comprehensive study of cultures all around the world confirmed that the desire to seek purpose, and to seek God and the afterlife, is deeply ingrained in human nature. Oxford University professor Roger Trigg was co-director of the three-year project that incorporated more than 40 different studies by dozens of researchers worldwide ... all of which came up with similar findings, including a widespread belief in some kind of afterlife, and an instinctive tendency to suggest that natural phenomena happen for a reason. "We tend to see purpose in the world," said Professor Trigg. "We see agency. We think that something is there even if you can't see it. [It's] a religious way of thinking ... **so deep-rooted in human nature, thwarting it is in some sense not enabling humans to fulfill their basic interests**," Trigg said [emphasis mine]. The longing for purpose, the study shows, is "universal, prevalent, and deep-rooted. It's got to be reckoned with. You can't just pretend it isn't there," he concluded.[70]

Be Fruitful and Grow

The existential, poetic ramblings of Ecclesiastes aside, the Bible does speak to what our purpose is: in Genesis, it says "Be fruitful and multiply." This refers to procreation, but even to the childless it implies a duty to **take care of the next generation**, plus a general mandate to be productive. Psychologist Erik Erikson and Theologian James Fowler (founder of the Center for Faith Development) both identified nurturing/teaching youngsters as a key, penultimate stage of psychosocial development.[71] This is why becoming parents, as much as finding productive careers, is quite fulfilling for most people. Both types of productivity meet a primal need.

The New Testament adds a different element, a spiritual and inwardly-personal Purpose. According to Jesus, our purpose is to kill our Selves! Do I have your attention now? Of course I don't mean *suicide*. The command to "die to Self" does not mean to kill the body, but to kill that false part of one's Self that is wholly egocentric. The purpose of this life is to learn how to rise above that selfish, cold heart, to try to crucify self until we become selfless — to exorcise our hate (or apathy) until we are full of love. In the next chapter, we will delve into more depth and detail regarding what "ego surrender" entails. Here let us now continue to speak about the Purpose of Life.

Inward and Outward Purpose

As we've seen, one problem with Purpose is that **outward** achievements — in the material "be fruitful" category — tend to be impermanent shrines to self-aggrandizement. It is, of course, a good and wonderful thing to build a hospital, church, college or even a successful business. But don't kid yourself: it will not last forever. Buildings and institutions, even the best of them, end up in the dustbin of history.

The other problem with Purpose is that even worthy **inward** efforts can devolve into selfish efforts. "Self-improvement" is also not a *bad* thing. But if all our efforts are directed inwardly, that seems more vice than virtue.

Scripture offers us a way out of this paradox by teaching us that one purpose of life is to **embrace Forgiveness.** Accept God's forgiveness. Extend forgiveness to others. Forgive one's self. These three practices may seem obvious and perhaps redundant, yet they are subtly different. The three elements of forgiveness are equally essential parts of the Purpose-filled Life; each must co-exist or the tripod falls. Let me explain.

A Tripod of Forgiveness on a Two-Way Street

The Gospels emphasize the three-fold nature of forgiveness again and again. Jesus actually described his own Purpose and Mission as one of "forgiveness of sins."[72] He told his disciples to forgive "70 times seven times" and "7 times 7," with the 7 being a symbolic number of perfection that equates to a *gazillion* times.[73] Perhaps the most important-yet-overlooked part of the forgiveness equation is that Jesus defines it as **a two-way street**. In the Gospel of Matthew, he states: "For if you forgive other people when they sin against you, your heavenly Father will also forgive you. But if you do not forgive others their sins, your Father will not forgive your sins."[74] Luke's gospel similarly records: "Do not judge, and you will not be judged. Do not condemn, and you will not be condemned. Forgive, and you will be forgiven."[75] And again in Luke 17:3, Jesus taught that if there is repentance by one who harmed you, you must forgive that person. **Human forgiveness must be reciprocal.** Even in the vital *Lord's Prayer*, Jesus instructed us to pray: "Forgive us as we forgive others."

Forgive ... Or Else?

The mutuality of forgiveness is not just a "suggestion" in Christian practice; it is a commandment with a threat. Matthew's gospel includes the Parable of the Unmerciful Servant, in which a freed slave who does not forgive the debts of another is thrown into jail to be tortured. Jesus uses the story to say, "So my heavenly Father will also do to every one of you, if you do not forgive your brother or sister from your heart."[76] This rare "threat" from Jesus is somewhat ameliorated by his prayer from the cross, "Abba, forgive them; for they do not know what they are doing."[77] Here Jesus offered unconditional forgiveness to his enemies. Not only had they had *not* forgiven him for his accused "crimes" nor *asked* for his forgiveness, but in fact, the enemies were still in the very process of torturing him! So, the emphasis here indicates a key to human-to-human forgiveness: while God offers Grace, Love and Forgiveness freely, for our own human sakes, forgiveness must be mutual and reciprocal! It is not that God withholds forgiveness; the point is, a non-forgiving heart is closed shut from receiving it.

The Third Element

What about the third element of forgiveness? It is less explicit, but it's there in the Gospels. To be an open receptacle, we must **forgive ourselves** ... or put another way, it is up to me to fully accept and internalize the forgiveness God extends to me. When the Disciple Peter had denied his association with Jesus three times, Jesus did not simply say, "You are forgiven." He asked Peter three times for an affirmation of loyalty and love. This "three for three" freed Peter from his guilt-ridden self-incrimination, and Peter went on to become a bold leader of the early Christian movement.

Jesus wanted us to have humility, but not by groveling. When John the Baptist said he was unfit to untie Jesus' sandals, Jesus rebuked him and submitted to be baptized by John. Likewise, when the disciples said they were unworthy to have Jesus wash their feet, he rebuked them — and washed their feet. The people of his time who were considered "low class" and "unclean" were also affirmed by Jesus: the tax collector, the adulteress, the Samaritan "woman at the well," etc. In Mark 12:31, he makes it clear that loving others does not mean hating self: "Love your neighbor as yourself." The reciprocity about love and forgiveness cannot be one-sided: love and forgive others, *and* love and forgive yourself (or more accurately, accept God's forgiveness for yourself).

It should be noted here that the need to accept forgiveness for oneself is not an endorsement of the modern "Self-esteem" movement. I seriously doubt that Jesus would sing along with Whitney Houston's hit song that proclaimed: "Learning to love yourself is the greatest love of all." No, it isn't. Self-sacrificial love of others is the greater love. Strangely, people who are plagued by guilt can still be narcissistic and overly prideful.

Relinquishing Ego to Receive Grace

Forgiving one's Self requires, paradoxically, a surrender of Ego ... or at least, of **False Ego**, a relinquishing of what mystic Eckhart Tolle calls "the pain body" (more on that in next chapter re: ego-release). Tied to the False Self is what I call "False Guilt." The pains of our past haunt us. Some of that is guilt or shame. If we have accepted God's forgiveness for our past, then any remaining sense of shame is a false-guilt. And some of that "pain body" aggravated by false guilt is ego-connected. Our ego-identity may be tied up in a martyr complex; we cling to the idea of injustice, we nurse our regrets and the unfairness of our past in part because we "get" something out of it. It is a paradox, an "unpleasant pleasure" or "unsatisfying gratification." Underlying it is an unwillingness to forgive the person(s) who harmed us, cheated us, treated us unfairly, or whatever. Freedom from the pain of our own guilt is blocked because we have not given pardon to the guilt of others.

This is not something God has inflicted on us. This is a law of the cosmos and a principle of the human psyche. You can't succeed in saying, "I had extenuating reasons for my sins and failures and flaws, so I deserve being forgiven," while at the same time, failing to extend the same consideration to others. I know it is hard. It is hard for me to let go and forgive the jerks of my past — some of them having acted quite selfishly or unfairly or even downright *evilly*. We do want justice ... but when we define justice as "they need to be punished for their sins," then we want justice for everyone but ourselves. True Justice is embodied in Christ's Golden Rule: "Treat others the same way you expect to be treated yourself."[78]

Letting Go of the Past

We have heard therapists speak of how to deal with our painful pasts. Some advice can go to extremes in either direction. Dwelling repeatedly on past pains is unwise; don't replay the "tape loop" of misery again and again. It is also unwise to "let go of the past" before we have dealt with it. They say "Forgive and forget," which is easier said than done. But it is even more difficult to "Forget and forgive." Forgiveness requires remembrance and contemplation first.

At some point, however, keep in mind the **Impermanence** of this reality. Nothing lasts. Our past is gone. It cannot truly be re-lived and certainly cannot be changed. What remains in our memory is only a shadow of the past. Even if a memory has not faded (which is doubtful), all memories are absolutely inaccurate, because we viewed the original event with our biased and myopic vision — and then stored it into memory cells with further self-benefitting "spin." Enjoy your photo albums. But let the past be what it is: passed.

Forgetting Assists Forgiveness

Eckhart Tolle was cited earlier ... not because I am a New Age devotee (I'm not), but because Tolle has offered some helpful thoughts on this topic, worth quoting here: "There is a fine balance between honoring the past and losing yourself in it. For example, you can acknowledge and learn from mistakes you made, and then move on and refocus on the now. It is called forgiving yourself."

This is the third leg of the forgiveness tripod. Forgiving self. If we can become humble yet honest enough with ourselves to let go of our neuroses, our self-pitying martyr complexes, and any unfair self-criticism, we open the door for the "free grace" God already has extended to us. This reciprocal tripod is not to say that God refuses to forgive if we don't forgive ourselves and others. More accurately, the fact is that God will not intrude and violate our free will. This is why Jesus said, "Behold, I stand at the door and knock. If anyone hears my voice and opens the door, I will come in …"[79]

You are Good (mostly!)

So much of modern religion emphasizes SIN. There is no benefit to "whitewashing" over sin; humanity has proven to be quite evil at times, and all of us are flawed. But the emphasis on sin over the last 50 years or so has not made America more virtuous. Probably the opposite. So, let's return to Early Christianity and its approach. One of the greatest of the Early Church founders and thinkers, Athanasius, taught the importance of these verses from Genesis: "So God created humankind in His image, in the image of God …" and "God saw everything that he had made, and indeed, it was very good."[80] Of course Athanasius understood this was before "the Fall" and "Original Sin" tainted the Garden. But the Fall did not erase the fact that **we are God's Good Creation**. Athanasius taught that humanity is like a Roman silver coin: at first, it was beautiful, new and perfect, imprinted with the image of its maker, Caesar. But over time, the world wears down the image, even to the point where the image may be blurred beyond easy recognition. Nevertheless, the coin still retains its value. And with Christ, we have a new imprinting, a fresh image of the face of God impressed upon us. Using the opposite of the Latin word that gives us "decapitate," Athanasius called it "recapitulation."[81]

Our Purpose: "Remember Who You Are"

God made us in God's image, the paragon of Creation. If the almighty and all-knowing God of the Universe designed you, and remains eager to love and accept you, I suspect it is okay to love and forgive yourself. It's not just *okay* — it's essential to our Purpose on earth. We are in the process of being redeemed and "recapitulated" via the *Imago Dei*.

Here again, an obstacle blinding us to the path forward may be past abuse, going all the way back to early childhood. Psychology and therapy can help. But the *theological* component, the spiritual dimension of forgiveness, is key. As with Athanasius, I'm less concerned with listing all of your sins or mine, and more concerned that we **remember who (and whose) we are**: made in the image of God.

Hellboy

Hellboy is a movie inspired by a Marvel comic book, the story of a child born in Hell, spewed out from Hades into our world, who becomes a superhero. Oddly, the movie is about the power of grace, and it begins and ends with a crucifix and cross. A crucifix statue looms over the title character's earthly arrival, a cross marks Hellboy, the cross saves him, and at the end of the movie, the grown-up Hellboy saves the world because of a cross. To be accurate, he was "saved" by the love of his adopted father, who had given a cross necklace to his Hades-born "son." In the final scene, the superhero seems to have been defeated by a demonic villain — bludgeoned into a semi-conscious state of amnesia. But then his friend hands him the cross necklace while telling him to "Remember who you are." The friend's words, and the necklace, remind Hellboy that his father's love had made him more human than demon. Cross in hand and remembering his "redeemed" identity, Hellboy stirs back to awareness and finds the strength to rebound and defeat the villain. Seriously, it's fun cinema and it's an allegory about Christian redemption. If even Hellboy can "remember" and be redeemed, perhaps so can we.

Do This in Remembrance

I can't seem to find the story of Hellboy in the Bible, ha, but many Bible passages do stress the importance of remembering our identity — that we are God's children. And something about the Hellboy story reminds me of an image from the older version of The Apostles' Creed, which says that Jesus "descended into Hell" (Also see 1st Peter 3:19–20.) A Greek Orthodox cathedral in Atlanta reflects that part of the creed, visually, with a ceiling mural of Jesus in Hell, grasping the hands of sufferers there, crouched and ready to leap out of the flames with them in tow.

Instead of dwelling on the negatives of your past, try to remember who you are and whose you are. We weren't spewed out of Hell; God created us in Paradise. We may have fallen, but Jesus calls us to remember our identity as God's Good Creation. The word "Christian" means to be "Christ-like." If you are a follower of another religion or a different creed, you will likely find similar teachings in your own faith. Becoming "like God" requires learning how to be humble, loving and forgiving. Those three things are a big chunk of our purpose on this planet, and attaining them is different than other achievements, in that they are by definition the opposite of ego-pursuits. Indeed, we don't so much "achieve" Christlikeness as "remember it" and "receive" it.

A Dynamite Chapter-Conclusion

Living life selfishly, without a purpose, is a terrible tragedy. Here's a story to illustrate. You have likely heard of Alfred Nobel, famous for establishing the Nobel Prizes for Peace, Medicine, Physics, etc. Nobel first became famous and successful as a chemist. He invented a useful household product called **dynamite**. He had envisioned his explosive as an aid to construction and mining ... which it was. But he was horrified to also see it used extensively in warfare.

Later in life, he picked up a newspaper and was shocked

to read his own obituary. A distant relative of the same name had died, and the press confused the deceased with the famous Alfred Nobel. The obituary mentioned the usual things, and then gave Nobel credit for the invention of dynamite, which, it said, was used in bombs. Nothing much good was printed about Alfred Nobel, and this forced him (the one still alive) to realize that for all his work and wealth, he had done almost nothing worthwhile. So, Nobel took productive action: using most of his accumulated wealth, he set up a trust fund and a perpetual committee to ensure that great achievements throughout history would be marked, and encouraged, by the Nobel Prize.

Maybe that, too, was an ego pursuit by Alfred Nobel. But it seems that his motivation was not to be rich or famous, as he had already achieved notoriety and wealth via his invention of dynamite. He wanted to give something *positive* back to the world. He made an effort to engage things beyond Self. Nobel left behind something bigger than his name. That's worth something.

All of this leads into our next chapter, as we sort out the paradox of Ego: True Self, False Self, and the tension between individuation (establishing a genuine identity) and ego-release.

Questions for Thought, Study and Group Discussion

If you are willing, share with someone else a few thoughts about what you envision your personal purpose(s) to be.

Imagine what your Obituary would say if you died tomorrow. Will you be satisfied with it?

How can we have a purposeful, meaningful life of achievement and yet still guard against Egoism?

Paradox 6

A thousand years from now, nothing of my earthly body will remain; but faith and the quantum view together suggest that my life has meaning and my existence shall endure in some form.

Reflective Quote for Chapter 6

The purposes of a person's heart are deep waters, but one who has insight draws them out.

~ *Proverbs 20:5*

Chapter 7

The Paradox of Ego χ Surrender

The kingdom of God is an upside-down kingdom. It beckons
us to gamble all ... to die so that we might live — to give our
lives away. Giving life away is a paradox. It's losing so we
can win. The kingdom of God means living that tension.
~ *Ken Wytsma, in* Pursuing Justice

Humility is, in a sense, admitting how egotistical you are.
~ *Criss Jami, Christian poet, author, musician*

Philosopher and surfboard designer Criss Jami (quoted above)
also said: "The biggest challenge after success is shutting up
about it." He seems to understand the unhealthy power of
a stoked and stroked ego. We should be quite cautious living
in a culture that makes a god out of Success and a religion of
Ego Worship. One modern magazine's title is emblematic of
our modern sickness — the popular mag is entitled: "Self." Our
self-orbiting society is commonly thrilled, but rarely fulfilled ...
constantly entertained, but never satisfied. We seem obsessed
with (to borrow the words of George Harrison) *I, Me, Mine.*
And the sad irony is, after decades digesting thousands of self-
help books and magazines, self-improvement courses, health
regimens and more, Americans are less healthy, more depressed,
and widely discontent. We have an opioid crisis and a suicide
epidemic ... and a spiritual malaise.

Culture of Narcissism
Professor and social critic Christopher Lasch nailed it a quarter-
century ago when his book title labeled us a "Culture of
Narcissism."[82] The dictionary defines narcissism as "self-love;

excessive interest in one's own appearance, comfort, importance, etc." I would call it a "love affair with mirrors." Excessive self-interest is the bane of American life in our times.

And yet, there is nothing new about it. Centuries ago, the Greek philosophers saw the absurdity of ego and thus spun the tale of mythological Narcissus. An extremely handsome young man-god, Narcissus was loved by a girl named Echo. But Echo's love for Narcissus was unrequited; he was so vainly in love with himself he could not return Echo's love. So, he was punished by the gods for his rejection of Echo, in this way: Narcissus came upon a placid pool and began gazing admiringly at his reflection. There he became transfixed by his own beauty for so long, he grew roots into the soil, and the gods turned him into a flower. Today, the Narcissus blossom is beautiful, but has little to say for itself.

The myth is interesting at several levels. First, the Narcissus story is where we get the word "narcissism." But it also shares the same Greek root-word, *narke*, from which we get the word "narcotic." "Narke" was Greek for numbness, stupor. Narcissus had fallen into a narcotic stupor induced by his own egomania. Let those with ears hear.

Famous Narcissists of the Bible

The Old Testament is filled with examples of narcissists: the Egyptian Pharaoh, who sacrificed his first-born rather than swallow his pride; King Saul, who was more concerned with popularity and praise than with what was best for the nation; Nebuchadnezzar, who built an immense statue to himself and forced everyone to worship his likeness; the vainglorious King Solomon, already mentioned … and so on.

The New Testament has its share of narcissists. "The woman at the well" serves as an example of a modern narcissist. Her conversation with Jesus revealed that she lived her life impulsively, having gone from man to man, despite living in a culture that discouraged promiscuity. She came to the well obsessively because she was thirsty ... not always for water, but for inner satiation. She had gone from one lover to another, trying to find fulfillment. She came partly to meet men at the well. (Wells served double-duty as a community hangout, and it's no coincidence that we refer to modern social bars as "the local watering hole.") As she listened to the words of Jesus, she came to realize there could be something deeper and more satisfying. Their conversation led to the statement that we must "worship in Spirit and in Truth."

And such is the human condition. We bounce from one craving to another hunger to yet another longing and even to addiction, never finding fulfillment in self and yet continuing to bow down in false worship at the altar of Narcissus.

Peyton Conway March wrote: "There is a wonderful law of nature that the three things we crave most in life — happiness, freedom, peace of mind — are always attained by giving them to someone else." It is a law of nature written into the fabric of the universe by our Creator, who is the opposite of Narcissus; God is a God of caring and giving and sharing.

Jesus and the Great Commandment

What did Jesus say about love? Many things. And one of the most famous is: "Love the Lord your God with all your heart and with all your soul and with all your mind. This is the first and greatest commandment. And the second is like it: Love your neighbor as yourself."[83] Before the Beatles said it, Jesus really did teach that love is all you need. For Jesus, the law of love summarized all the words of the Law and the Prophets who had come before. Listen how Jesus defined love: "Greater love has no one than this, that he lay down his life for his friends."[84] Love, in the Christian worldview, is inseparable from *self-sacrifice*. If we are not self-sacrificing, we are not truly "loving neighbor." As Dr. Martin Luther King put it, "The true neighbor will risk his position, his prestige and even his life for the welfare of others."[85]

That's a high order. In our culture, the word "love" is so tangled up with sex and pleasure that for many folks, saying "I love you" has as much spiritual value as pronouncing "I love ice cream." **True** love is a decision, a commitment to a set of selfless actions. Or as the rock group Boston sang, it's "More than a feeling." Love, according to Jesus, is not emotion, but *action* — a series of decisions to do what is good, right and true. We confuse true love with a lust for superficial beauty, rather than a commitment to substance. Poet John Donne wrote, "Love built on beauty, soon as beauty, dies." Perhaps he had Narcissus in mind.

Mature Views on Love

According to legend, an elderly Apostle John, lacking the strength to walk, had to be carried to the pulpit by his disciples to preach. His "sermons" became only six words long: "Love one another, love one another." John did not attribute his brevity to frailty. He later explained: "There is nothing else: attain love, and you have enough."

The early church father Augustine spoke similar sentiments: "Love God and do as you please." All of these sources echo the main message of the Messiah: "Love God and love neighbor."

It does seem that the more luxurious and comfortable our lives become, the more inclined we are, paradoxically, to selfishness. In times of hardship and struggle we find the human spirit breaking free of narcissism — times not common to our twenty-first century. James Herriot, in his book *All Creatures Great and Small*, wrote about a widow named Mrs. Dalby, who lived through the hard-scrabble years of the Great Depression. She had lost her husband when her boys were young, but rather than despair, endured years of hard labor to keep the infertile farm going as she raised her children single-handed. As James Herriot sat in her kitchen sharing tea one day, the frail Mrs.

Dalby glanced at a picture of her long-dead husband on the mantle and remarked:

"'It would have been our thirtieth anniversary today.'"

Herriot tells what happened next: "I looked up at her, surprised. She never spoke of such things, and I didn't know how to answer. I couldn't very well say, 'Congratulations' when she had spent twenty of those years alone ...

"'Yes, thirty years,' Mrs. Dalby said, looking slowly around the room, her face serious. 'Mr. Herriot,' she began, and I was sure that at last, on this special day, she was going to [justifiably whine and complain] about the years of struggle, the nights of worry and tears, the grinding toil. 'Mr. Herriot,' she said with a gentle smile, 'are you quite sure that the tea is to your liking?'"[86]

The Kudzu of Narcissism

In case you missed the point, that's a story of "anti-narcissism." Mrs. Dalby refused to drown in self-pity. In our society, we choke on selfishness and self-absorption. Narcissus is not a flower, but a weed ... a weed which grows in the garden of souls. To amplify the metaphor, this is no ordinary weed. This is kudzu! If you are not familiar with this irrepressible spreading vine, I'll interject an old joke: How do you plant kudzu? Dig a two-inch hole, drop in a kudzu seed ... and run! Similarly, narcissism is running rampant in America, and yes, I find it in the garden of my own soul.

If raging narcissism invades your garden like kudzu, it requires eternal vigilance and constant trimming back. In contrast, Jesus said in Matthew 16:24, "If anyone would come after me, he must deny himself and take up his cross and follow me." This challenge was given by a man-god who anticipated his own torturous death by crucifixion. Christ battled Narcissus in pain and prayer, saying to the Godhead: "Yet not my will, but thine." In the ultimate sacrifice and final denial of the ego-self at Golgotha, something powerful and mysterious happened with the universe. Narcissus was defeated. The dark spirits of pagan mythology along with the dark impulses of the human soul were trampled. Jesus was victorious. He returned from the dead with a new flesh, transformed and purified into a new creature ... offering us a new hope.

What this Means for Us: The Tightrope of Ego

Most of the major religions teach us to **surrender Ego**. Self-denial is not only difficult, but the call to surrender also begs the question of what "Ego" means. From a psychological viewpoint, even pioneers of the term — Freud and Jung — could not agree on the definition. Jung's definition applies the word Ego to a portion of the Self: our decision-making consciousness that chooses and interacts with the most relevant information from the environment. The ego is, in part, the social self; it's how "I" relate to the external world, according to Dr. Jung. He had a more holistic and spiritual notion of the Self than did Freud, and preferred to use and explore the Greek word, *psyche*, or *self*, rather than dissecting things into Ego, Superego and Id, as Freud famously did. Jung wrote: "By psyche I understand the totality of all psychic processes, conscious as well as unconscious."[87]

Herein I use an amalgam of Jung, Freud and Erik Erikson's work, and loosely speak of Ego as the Self, the "I" (which is, of course, what *ego* means in Latin). But we may find it more helpful to speak of our True Self versus a False Self; for many folk the True Self is sleeping ("spiritually unconscious"), leaving the False Self in control — self-deceived yet self-centered "Egoism."

Eckhart Tolle describes the difference between the two: "Most people are still completely identified with the incessant stream of mind, of compulsive thinking, most of it repetitive and pointless. There is no 'I' [or true self/ego] apart from their thought processes and the emotions that go with them. This is the meaning of being spiritually unconscious [what Tolle calls the "pain-body"]." Tolle continues: "[Conversely,] some people never forget the first time they dis-identified from their [false] thoughts and thus briefly experienced the shift in identity from being the content of their mind to being the awareness in the background [thus glimpsing the True Self]. For others it happens in such a subtle way they hardly notice it, or they just notice an influx of joy or inner peace without knowing the reason."[88]

Is Ego-Release Truly the Better Life?

Most spiritual teachers, in various ways, tell us that **contentment comes only when we lose false-ego desires**. Our contemporary society ("pop-culture") has rejected that. The commercial world — especially Madison Avenue advertisers and celebrity-worshiping TV shows — have tried to convince us of the opposite: that if we just get enough material goodies, or enough fame, or enough status, we will be happy. Despite the majority of US citizens identifying themselves as "Christian," the US has placed Individualism ahead of Community. Early Christianity now looks quite foreign in contrast, as they preached of the vital importance of **community** (see *oikos* and *ekklesia*, in New Testament terms) and lived a communitarian lifestyle alien to modern capitalism.

You would think people would listen to Jesus, or Buddha, or Krishnamurti, or even Tolle — teachers whose lifestyles embodied sacrifice — rather than follow the advice of shallow shysters trying to divide us to profit from us. But all the signs point to this diagnosis: **we are an ego-driven culture, and concurrently, a splintered, isolated, depressed, anxious, addicted and unhappy society.**

If folks won't listen to Jesus, perhaps science can convince. In his interesting book, *Lost Connections*, Johann Hari emphasizes that healthy communities are essential to personal health and happiness. Hari refers to a wide-range of **scientific studies** that confirm what spiritual teachers have long taught regarding the importance of escaping the tyranny of individualistic, egocentric pursuits. Hari reports that over 22 studies "found that the more materialistic and extrinsically motivated you become, the more depressed you will be."[89] By the phrase "materialistic and extrinsic motivations," he means the all-too-common individualistic pursuit of trophies, trinkets, toys and ego aggrandizement. He added, "There's strong evidence that we all get the most pleasure from [being in] what are called 'flow states' — moments when we simply lose ourselves doing something we love and are carried along in the moment."[90] "Flow states" are times when we break free from the false ego.

Similarly, altruistic efforts — caring about and serving others instead of our Selves — yield greater contentment than self-centered actions. Hari calls these "intrinsic goals, like being a better friend or a more loving son or a better piano player [for the sheer joy of it, not to win applause]."[91] After studying cultures around the world and digesting scores of scientific studies, Hari concluded that escaping the tyranny of ego to become socially connected is the only way to escape unhappiness. "If you want to stop being depressed, don't be you. Don't be your [false] self ... Be **us**. Be **we**. Be part of the group. The real path to happiness ... comes from dismantling our ego walls ... [and] letting yourself flow into other people's stories."[92]

The best scientific research (in psychology, sociology and biology) is now confirming what the best religious wisdom has been teaching for centuries.

Pure Immortal Diamond

The False Self is the narcissistic ego, fed by external artificialities. The False Self is rooted in self-deception. I appreciate, but differ slightly with, Friar Richard Rohr, who seems too quick to say that the False Self is not "bad." I've observed that the False Self *is* a source for all kinds of bad things: evil, fear, conflict, etc. But I do love Rohr's thoughts and writing, particularly his definition of the True Self as "strong, true, clear, but hidden within us" like an "immortal diamond."[93] Rohr borrowed the phrase from the poetry of Gerard Manly Hopkins, and *immortal diamond* may be another name for the "luminous, clear (or white) stone" Jesus mentioned in Revelation 2:17. (We will explore the meaning of that curious verse before this chapter ends.)

One purpose of this life is to become a mature, genuine, self-aware, individuated identity. *Individuation* (not be confused with *Individualism*) is described by C. G. Jung as a noble journey of the psyche, a process of moving toward wholeness and becoming more fully conscious of one's self as a unique human being. The aim is to do so with humility, so the search to be mature and unique does not mean becoming "superior" to others. Yet our ultimate aim *is* spiritual perfection, the Immortal Diamond.

Our Journey's Destination

The True Self is at once our innermost or utmost being, our essential real "me" as created by God and seen by God at our best ... *and* it is a future Ideal Self that we grow into, the destination of our spiritual journey. The Ideal Self is what Jesus meant by his command, "Be ye perfect." Despite the high expectations of Jesus (and Methodism's founder, John Wesley), I have never observed perfection being attained fully in *this* lifetime by any mere mortal. Nevertheless, we can set it as a goal and move closer toward our True Self, as we bring our False Ego under the control of humility.

I write not as an expert on humility, but as one who has foolishly sought fame and acclaim — an expert on fool's pride. I don't float serenely like a lotus blossom and give smug platitudes on how you can achieve nirvana. I'm not there yet. I struggle with the tyranny of my own ego as much as anyone else. While trying to "grow up" and become a worthy, unique individual, I've had to ask myself, "How can I find my identity, worth and purpose without over-inflating the False Self?" We tiptoe at the edge of the abyss of Narcissism. Even self-examination, if it involves too much self-focus, may tip us over the edge.

Perhaps a surrender of the ego is easy for some ... for people who have been trampled by life's travails, whose self-worth and self-identity has been worn down to a wisp. But for most humans, the ego or false self — with its self-protective instinct, its myopic narcissism — is a hard nut to crack, a fine line to walk ... a tightrope. Use whatever metaphor you wish: the marathon of self-surrender is never run quickly; the prison of pride is not easily escaped. Pride is the brick wall blocking us from the "Garden of Allah," blocking us from contentment, from learning and growth, from deep and lasting relationships. To continue my metaphor party, egocentrism is the fountainhead of troubled waters, a source of anger and conflict that flows from our desire for dominance. And this is the first step in surrendering ego: realizing how evil and ugly it can be.

Ego, the Destroyer

None of this is new to those familiar with the Bible. Original Sin began, according to Genesis, with the pride of the Serpent infecting Eve and Adam, in this temptation to self-aggrandizement: "Ye can be gods." Some have even suggested it was God's original plan ... that for humans to become fully sentient, fully conscious — and to have Free Will — we would *have* to have eaten of the Tree of Knowledge of Good and Evil. Whether God's plan or not, the reality now is this: Ego development, death and rebirth are necessary components of the human experience. Here again, we find paradox. As mentioned in my first chapter, even the symbol of Sin and the Fall has a paradoxical title: the Tree of the Knowledge of *Good and Evil*. The entire story is filled with paradoxes: the Creation of humans was immediately followed with their encounter with Destruction (Mortality).

In Hindu mythology, the gods Brahma and Shiva also embody this connection between Creation and Destruction on the fulcrum of Ego ... another form of paradox. The Creator god,

Brahma, and the Destroyer, Shiva, are locked in a struggle — in some versions, Shiva embodies both creation and destruction in a single incarnation of the paradox of creation and consciousness. Only by destroying the old could Shiva pave the way for a new creation.

Maya (Deceptive Illusion)

Albert Einstein referred to the Ego as "an optical illusion of consciousness." The False Self is both a vaporous illusion and a real thing. The False Self is *Maya* (the illusory, self-deluded miasmic ego), a palpable artifice, a constructed identity cobbled together of past experiences, neuroses, emotional "needs" and physical cravings. The False Self is rooted in the physical body and in the material world and in our social/cultural environs. Here I caution the reader not to think dualistically; I'm not saying the material world is all evil and the spiritual world is all good. Asceticism is misplaced devotion. It helps no one. Moreover, asceticism can, itself, become an ego pursuit and a point of boasting. As the Apostle Paul put it, such physical disciplines are of "little value."[94] Genesis tells us at the get-go that Creation is Good. The Bible asserts that we humans, in particular, are a sacred creation, made just a tad lower than the angels; we are the sixth-day pinnacle, the paragon of earthly creatures. At times, Paul seems tempted to embrace asceticism ... but in the end, rejects it as an insult to the body, which he calls a "temple."[95] The paradox in all this is that Jesus still calls us to deny Self, to ultimately sacrifice the False Self, to metaphorically burn it on the altar. Of course, the ritual of self-sacrifice is difficult.

Pride/Hubris

What I've written above is rather abstract. The Bible moves quickly to **pragmatic application**: Day by day, the challenge of proper Ego rebirth is understood best using the single word, **Pride**. The New Testament was written in Greek, and the ancient

Greeks had a more precise and descriptive word for this vice: *Hubris*. As Americans, we tend to use "pride" as a positive: be proud of your team, proud of your country, proud of your children. Forget that aspect/definition. The Bible speaks of Hubris as extreme pride, egoistic ambition, pomposity and arrogance. For the classical Greeks, Hubris was often a plot theme in Greek plays (usually tragedies), a character flaw often seen even in *heroes*, like Oedipus and Achilles. From such morality plays we get the familiar aphorism, "Pride goeth before a fall."

The lesson is woven as a seamless tapestry across later history and literature. Chaucer's *Canterbury Tales* portrays the character Pride leading the parade of vices; thus, Pride literally went first ... before the other failings. In real life, overinflated egos have preceded the fall of many an accomplished leader ... from Napoleon at Waterloo to Nixon at Watergate. The dangers of outsized egos are warned of in ancient fables, from the Tower of Babel, to the Greek myth of Icarus soaring to the sun where his ego was singed along with his feathers, to Aesop's Fables of small, meek animals triumphing over the haughtiness of the big and strong. It's a universal truth ... universally ignored.

Taming Reptiles

After recognizing the ugliness of ego and hubris, the second step in escaping from the tyranny of the false self is realizing, and coping with, **the connection between fear and ego**. The false ego is tied to our animal survival instinct; astrophysicist Carl Sagan called it the mindless, instinctive "reptilian brain." Because fear is animalistic, deeply-rooted and reflexive, it is difficult to tame.

My cousin owns an alligator farm and zoo. (Wes Moore is actually famous, having been featured many times on the TV show, *Animal Planet*.) He has some 500 gators in his complex, and interacts with dozens daily. When I watch Wes do his gator show, his confidence and calm around them can mislead you. They are not tame. You can tame a lion, but you cannot tame an alligator. As Wes says, "Alligators are predictable animals. They *will* bite you. It's what they are designed to do."

Back to taming the false ego: the ego has a role in protecting us. Children, in particular, need **ego boundaries** to keep them safe in this world. But since the false ego seems to have the tiny, instinctual brain of an alligator, it can mindlessly bite us. Identifying and controlling the false ego can be difficult and dangerous. Caution is called for. Paradoxically, ego-release only comes via courage. This is where religion can be of assistance, as long as our spiritual framework itself isn't rooted in fear. Ideally, our belief system is built on a trust in God, who gives us confidence in the face of fear. We covered this topic already in the chapter on fear and God's love. I would just add here that the less confident we are in some form of afterlife the greater grip fear and false ego may have on us.

Escape from the Ego: the Eastern Exit

For this reason, some resist the ego-dissolution practices found in Buddhism and Hinduism, as they offer less assurance of the eternal survival of a conscious Self. The Ego (False or True) doesn't find comfort in the idea of eventually disappearing mindlessly into the sea of Brahman. According to Buddhism scholar David Loy, our fear of ego-less-ness may be even stronger than our fear of death.[96] Speaking of the process of escaping ego and the related fear, Professor Loy wrote: "It's like peeling off the layers of an onion. When you get to the end, nothing is left ... [But] we don't *like* being nothing. A gaping hole at one's core is quite distressing. [And if] my constructed sense of self is ungrounded, it is haunted by a basic sense of ... insecurity."[97]

Springing from Hinduism, Buddhism sought a way out of the ego trap. Zen Buddhism teaches the need for Ego-death by learning (mainly via meditation) to "forget" the accumulated encrustations of false ego. The subject of ego-death in Zen is more complex than I have room to describe here, but suffice it to say that it is not calling for complete obliteration of the Self-Identity or personal consciousness. Buddhist Enlightenment occurs when the seeker stops walking blindly and reactively through life ... and though it may feel like a "death" or a falling into the void, once accomplished, the seeker finds liberation from false ego and discovers his or her true self. You've heard the expression (from Psalm 30), "Joy comes in the morning." To turn the phrase, joy comes in the *mourning* ... only after mourning the death of one's false ego. As Professor of Asian Religion Jin Park puts it, the one who finds Nirvana may say: "I become nothing, and discover that I am everything ... and can be anything."[98]

Escape from the Ego: the Christian Mystics' Exit

Christian teaching on this matter exists at two levels. The literal or overt level is **outward self-denial**, the adoption of the servant way of life (charity, love, selflessness, virtue). This is sometimes misconstrued as asceticism, turned into a pummeling of the flesh or trying to emulate Jesus' agony, to "walk the stations of the cross." Many well-loved Christian hymns ask us to be crucified with Jesus. Hopefully, that's meant metaphorically. I'm not up to being tortured and nailed to a cross, frankly.

But the other, deeper level is waiting there in the Scriptures to be discovered. The thoughtful Christian mystics already found it: **we can spiritually transcend Ego to find union with God**. The mystic's approach still involves a process of killing off as much of the false ego as possible. St. John of the Cross, the sixteenth-century Spanish mystic, wrote of ego-transcendence this way: "Swiftly, with nothing spared, I am being completely dismantled." Dionysius (the Christian mystic, not the Greek philosopher) said that we must first renounce the false ego and all the trappings of the physical world. Then it is possible to be "drawn upward" to the "ray of divine darkness," to divine mystery that "surpasses all existence."[99] Also consider the life and writing of the Carmelite nun and mystic, St. Teresa of Ávila.

A better Christian saint would be hard to find, yet the Church tried her for heresy (maybe the reader understands why I have some ambivalence toward orthodoxy!). She had mystical visions of God and was able to escape her earthly soul/ego — yet this was not an instant or easy journey. She described enlightenment or spiritual "bliss" as a 7-level, arduous process. She wrote that "... self-knowledge is indispensable ... Nothing else, however elevated, perfects the soul, which must never seek to forget its own nothingness. Let humility be always at work, like the bee at the honeycomb, or all will be lost. But remember, the bee leaves its hive to fly in search of flowers, and the soul [must] cease thinking of itself to rise in meditation on the grandeur and majesty of its God. It will learn its own baseness [humility] better thus than by self-contemplation, and will be freer ..."[100]

A Note about Children and Ego

A quick aside, at the risk of stating the obvious: as children and young persons, the emergence of our egos seems necessary. They are not ready to be taught ego-obliteration (although they can certainly be instructed on the virtues of humility). The consciousness and personality of the Self/Ego can be a healthy and natural growth process in children, necessary for the eventual maturation toward the True Self. Young persons **need** affirmation, self-esteem, feelings of competence and self-confidence. But in the West, we go overboard with that, awarding trophies and prizes for the slightest participation in a skill. Where does it end? Celebrities, with a Peter Pan never-grow-up syndrome, are never satisfied with their multitude of award shows — Oscars, Emmy's, Golden Globes, People's Choice Awards, *ad nauseum*. Ultimately, the inflated Ego must pop like a balloon. This should not happen to little children, who need unconditional love and affirmation; the balloon-popping should only happen to adults who *act* like children.

Bury the Seed to See it Grow

The false ego must die in order for the New/True Self to be born. This is why John records Jesus' interesting phraseology: "You must be born again,"[101] and that "unless a grain of wheat falls into the earth and dies," it amounts to nothing ... but if it "dies" and is buried/planted, "it bears much fruit."[102] Jesus warned us against sin in order to help us crack the ego. Sin is the negative side of the equation; humility and love are the positive side. Jesus modeled this. His person, the life story of Christ, is that of the Upside-down King: a king born not in golden splendor but in an animal barn; a king who rode in his triumphal processional upon a comic baby-donkey; a king whose crown was a wreath of thorns.

The Apostle Paul wrote about this ego-death (and ensuing renewal). First, in Philippians 2, Paul described it in a passage called the "Kenosis of Christ," from the Greek word "κενόω" — the self-emptying of Jesus' divine power, will and ego, to submit to sacrificial death on the cross: "Christ Jesus, ... being in very nature God, did not consider equality with God something to be used to his own advantage; rather, he made himself nothing [Greek κενόω = "emptied himself"] by taking the very nature of a servant, being made in human likeness. And being found in appearance as a mortal, he humbled himself by becoming obedient to death — even death on a cross."[103] Second, in reference to you and me, Paul called for our own kenosis: "Lay aside the old self, which is [deceived and] corrupted ... Be renewed in the spirit of your mind, and put on the new self."[104]

The New Self or re-born person is a concept found throughout the New Testament, from Matthew to the Book of Revelation. The Christian concept of ego-escape is, to my mind, more reassuring than in some religions. Superficially reading Eastern religions, one may get the wrong notion that conquering the False Self — ego-release — is achieved purely through mental exercises and some kind of "one and done" Eureka moment. The Christian perspective clarifies that spiritual enlightenment is meaningless if it is not manifest in the physical world, by a posture of servanthood. Jesus made this clear with his example in John 13. He knelt on the floor before his disciples and washed their dirty feet. In a society with strict rules about handling things unclean, it was significant that their "Lord/Master" did this. He then said: "Now that I, your Lord and Teacher, have washed your feet, you also should wash one another's feet. I have set you an example that you should do as I have done for you."[105] He was not establishing a liturgical ritual; he was showing them the discipline of service. This was a visible example of "the posture of humility." Kneeling to serve others is also the posture of enlightenment.

Summary

Fear drives out love. But arrogance drives out true spirituality. Jesus addressed this with another paradox, saying *the least among us shall turn out to be the greatest*. Humility equates to true greatness. Jesus was not a lone voice on this matter. Confucius said, "Humility is the solid foundation of all virtues." Muhammad said: "Be humble, and Allah will exalt you." Benjamin Franklin's 13-point plan for living virtuously listed the final/highest virtue as Humility, summarized by the simple statement: "Imitate Jesus and Socrates." The best of wisdom found in religion and philosophy points to this truth: **Surrendering ego in exchange for humility is the key to love, grace and fulfillment.** True religion *requires* humility ... and *engenders* it.

God did not create us as mere momentary foam on the ocean, only to melt back into the faceless ocean. The goal is to become something better, a new and transcendent Self but still in possession of our genuine core identity. As mentioned, some call it the Immortal Diamond (the Gnostics called it "The Pearl of Great Price"). This is hinted at in Revelation's picture of the afterlife, where Jesus says: "To the one who overcomes [sin and death], I will bestow on that person's Self a secret nourishment, and a luminous stone [or jewel] with a new name engraved upon it, known only to the one who receives it."[106] The Greek word used there for a *new* name is καινός, which means emphatically new: "new in species or character, or mode, renovated, better, of higher excellence."[107] The New but still True Self. This is what Jesus called the "higher righteousness," the luminous Self of spiritual truth.

Let me close this chapter with the words of Father Alfonse Nazzaro: "The Lord is calling us to holiness through humility. The Beatitudes are the wakeup call, the call to arms, for all those who wish to fall into His arms ... He proves over and over again that wealth and power have nothing, absolutely nothing, to do with holiness. In fact, they are an obstacle. [As Jesus said:] 'Whoever wishes to lose his life for my sake, will gain it.'"[108]

Questions for Thought, Study and Group Discussion

Rhetorical question: Is it more difficult for people in ego-ballooning positions (a CEO, a millionaire, a celebrity, etc.) to be aware of the False Self? Discuss.

A follow-up to that discussion: If you are a member of a religious denomination, church, sect, synagogue, or such, describe your ecclesiastical hierarchy. Do we put our "spiritual leaders" on pedestals or adorn them with power in ways that sabotage their ego-health?

If humility is a posture and action, what are some actions (and/or spiritual disciplines) a person might take to reel in his or her over-extended ego?

Paradox 7

Finding one's Self comes by losing ego; freedom comes via surrender.

Reflective Quote for Chapter 7

Seek freedom and become captive of your desires. Seek discipline and find your liberty.

~ *Frank Herbert, Novelist, in Chapterhouse*

Chapter 8

The Paradox of Love χ Punishment (Hell)

Has God created millions of people ... who are going to spend eternity in anguish? Can God do this, or even *allow* this, and still claim to be a loving God?
~ Rob Bell, Christian author and evangelical pastor

It's not a question of God "sending" us to Hell. In each of us there is something growing up which will of itself be Hell unless it is nipped in the bud ... [T]he damned are ... successful rebels to the end, [but] the doors of hell are locked from the inside.
~ C. S. Lewis, Christian author and professor

In the previous chapter, we again considered how crucial it is to be freed from fear in order to grow in spiritual maturity and find one's True Self. For some, a big *religious* fear remains within this quandary: How could a loving God condemn persons to Hell? Conversely, how could a God of Justice permit Hitler and his ilk to go unpunished? If ignored, this paradox erodes our trust in God's love.

The Hell, You Say?

The scholarly magazine, *Christian History*, reminds us that there has never been unanimous agreement on what Hell is or who might go there. The magazine summarizes three historical positions, or categories of thought, on the topic of punishment in the Afterlife: **Traditional, Conditional** and **Universalist.**[109] Let's consider each.

The Traditional View of Hell

If you were raised in a Catholic or Baptist Church, you likely were taught what the magazine labels a "Traditional" belief: that anyone who is not "saved" will be judged at death and sentenced to eternal condemnation, to a Hell defined as a place of endless, agonizing torture. Setting aside the Catholic notion of Purgatory (because it is merely a waiting room, and a person might still go from there to a fiery Hades), a Traditional view is that once a person is in Hell, there is no exit. But even that category has sub-categories. The revered, orthodox theologian, C. S. Lewis, can be counted in the "Traditional" camp ... yet even he leaves the door open to the idea that Hell might *leave the door open* (see Lewis' quote, above).

The Traditional stance has, unfortunately, become the most prevalent among American Christians. I say "unfortunate" because the idea that a Loving God sentences people to everlasting torture has driven more people away from faith than any other doctrine.

Set aside whatever fear or indoctrination you may have had and consider the case of Jack. Fictional Jack was a 14-year-old boy, raised (and abused) by alcoholic parents. He had never heard any substantial information about Jesus or salvation or how to attain it. Out of the pain he experienced in his home life, he sought comfort in smoking pot, shoplifting candy bars, and ogling his nubile female classmates in gym class. When caught in a petty theft, he lied about it to his parents, "dishonoring" them. So, in a year's time, Jack had violated over half of the Ten Commandments! At the end of his year of teenage rebellion, he died of Leukemia. According to the Traditional view, Jack would then stand before the throne of our Loving God, who might say, "Sorry, Jack, even though you are just a child and — excuse the pun — *you don't know Jack* about life, you are past the age of accountability. So, because of your bad choices, I'm going to toss you into a Lake of Fire, where you will suffer excruciating pain for 1,000 years. Or maybe for eternity, I'm not sure. So, anyway, have a nice day!"

Does Traditional = Rational?

First, let me assure you I am not putting words in God's mouth nor being irreverent; I don't believe for a minute that God would actually say anything like that false "Jack" scenario. Yet, after removing the humor I inserted, **that is exactly what the Traditional Doctrine of Hell proposes for Jack's destiny!** The purveyors of such a doctrine are themselves irreverent, because they portray God as unloving and unjust. The absurdity of it is mind-boggling: for one year of adolescent bad choices, Jack would receive a thousand years of agonizing torture? The Traditional Doctrine usually that God is ruled by the need for cosmic Justice (as if God were hidebound by a Law of Retributive Punishment). But could there be any scenario more unjust? I couldn't bear even an *hour* of unceasing pain by fire, much less an eternity of it.

How do Traditionalists Answer the Imbalance?

So how do the Traditionalists deal with this huge imbalance of justice? Mostly they try not to address the issue at all. When forced, they have two answers: Jesus and the cross save us from that pit of Hell, and those who are not saved "made their own choices." They say things like, "God is grieved when a sinner goes to Hell." Yet, we are to believe that the Almighty can't lift a finger to save His precious child screaming in the flames? That would be a weak and callous god. Did Jack have any chance to do otherwise in his miserable short life? We might reasonably ask how Jack "chose" agonizing Hell over embracing a loving God, when that loving God never stood before Jack and said, "Jack, I love you. Please follow me so you don't fall into that Lake of Fire over there." No, according to the Traditional view, the first time Jack meets his Loving God, God is seated on a throne with a judge's gavel and offers no choice to Jack. He mandates only a torture-sentence. Finesse it however you wish, the Traditional doctrine is horrible, irrational and inconsistent with the God we see revealed in Jesus Christ (forgiving and loving).

Why would someone believe such absurdity? Often, it is because they cannot see past their strictly literalistic approach to Scripture. They refuse to understand that the (few) verses in Scripture that speak of Hell (*Gehenna* or Hades) or a Lake of Fire might be metaphorical, or in the case of Jesus' teachings, a form of hyperbolic Jewish wit.

I Am Not a Lone Outlier

In my lifetime, authors who challenge the conservative-traditionalist view of Hell have been accused of being radical, atheistic liberals or outlying rogues. This is unfair and inaccurate. In my case, I am generally an orthodox Christian ... and not alone in my hesitations regarding divine punishment. A partial review of Christian history may bring perspective to this subject:

Clement of Alexandria (c. 150–215 CE) was a devout "early Christian father" who wrote (in Greek) about the concept of an *apokatastasis*, the return of all created beings to God. He also suggested that the fire of judgment likely refers to a refining fire of purification rather than destruction or torture.

Irenaeus, Bishop of Lyons, (c. 120–203 CE) is well known for his refutation of the heretical Gnostics. But he also had a grace-filled understanding of salvation, stressing Jesus' redemption of humanity as a *whole*, with some form of Hades as a place only for those who insistently choose to live apart from God. (Incidentally, not everyone of the ancient world believed the world was flat; Irenaeus referred to the Earth as a sphere.)

Origen (c. 184–254 CE) was a fervent Christian who wrote quite a bit about eschatology (i.e. how the world will end, and the disposition of souls at the Final Judgment). Origen believed in a divine initiative to restore created minds/spirits back to their pristine state, as God had originally created them. This world, in Origen's view, is a "purgatorial discipline," a school for fallen souls, created by God in order to help return us to Paradise. In this view, Hell is simply an extreme form of that purgatorial discipline, and verses warning of eternal punishment are actually benevolent deceptions by God, aimed at motivating us. Like Clement, Origen believed in the *apokatastasis*, the final restoration of all creation.

Athanasius, (296–373 CE), became a revered Christian patriarch in Alexandria, and a strong defender of orthodoxy — especially regarding the Incarnation of Christ. Athanasius wrote of an eventual restoration of Paradise and re-creation of the human spirit, where we will be set free (by Christ's redemptive power) from our "fallen" condition and again have perfect union with the divine Creator. Athanasius, like many other bishops, also could not accept that God would purposely torture humans for eternity; perhaps, at most, those who are determined to reject God may drift toward nothingness. (A view later suggested in C. S. Lewis' fictional imagining of Heaven and Hell, *The Great Divorce*.) We will return to Athanasius' ideas momentarily.

Other stalwart "church fathers and mothers" who believed in either Universalism or some form of *Apokatastasis* or a Recapitulation of All Creation include Didymus, Saint Anthony, Pamphilus Martyr, Methodius, St. Gregory of Nyssa and his sister, Saint Macrina, Evagrius Ponticus, Diodore of Tarsus, Saint Jerome, Cassian, Maximus the Confessor ... the list goes on.

Universalism and Heresy?

Despite it being quite common in the first 500 years of Christendom to believe that all humans would be universally saved, later church councils dismissed the doctrine of "Universalism" as heresy. Lumping all unorthodox theologies about the afterlife into the category of Universalism is lazy shorthand. I don't believe for a moment that God is a torturer, but of course I do not know what will ultimately happen to people who simply refuse to have communion with their Creator. And frankly, I'm not eager to share Heaven with Adolf Hitler and other mass murderers. Honest Christians can disagree on this issue, but they cannot claim to know the details of the Afterlife as dogmatic fact. Trust and faith do not require that we know all the answers to the mystery.

Of This I Am Confident ...

I do have a Creed, and hold as true many specific points of doctrine. But there is one thing I cannot accept: God as a masochistic torturer. If Orthodoxy insists upon the idea of eternal torture, count me a heretic. Sinners writhing for eons in pain and fiery despair most assuredly **cannot be reconciled with this key part of Orthodoxy: that Yahweh is a Just and Loving God**. Christ is first and foremost a Redeemer, and only secondarily a Judge.

As the Bible makes clear, the Judeo-Christian God will apply justice not just *fairly*, but actually with *leniency*. Does Orthodoxy really want to claim that a person who lived an unselfish life filled with sincere altruism would still be tortured with fire, relentlessly for all eternity, punished for the "sin" of not accepting doctrinal formulas about Jesus Christ? If you follow literalism, inerrancy and orthodoxy to their bitter conclusion, you would be saying to a terminal cancer patient, perhaps a 12-year-old Hindu boy in Mumbai, taking his last gasp of air: "Because you did not pray the Sinner's Prayer, and did not verbally accept Christ as Lord and Savior ... you are now going to spend eternity in sheer agony, burning in flames forever. PS: God loves you!"

Not even my affinity for applying paradox can fix that

dysfunctional clash of "truths."

God Does Not Foreclose

David Lowes Watson, in his controversial book, *God Does Not Foreclose*, wrote about both the idea of God inflicting eternal torture on sinners, and the collective evil and suffering in the world. Watson concludes that "... if so much evil can be visited on so many innocent people ... then the justice of God cannot be an impartial, objective, legal system." Watson continued: "The only possible way out of this legal 'Catch-22' is to remember that is now how God's justice works; that God is a God of saving-righteousness, not forensic judgement."

Yes, Jesus made a few references in the New Testament to Hades/Gehenna ... but these are in the context of parables that were clearly "mythic," hyperbolic stories intended to illustrate a larger point. While other biblical references to some form of "Hell" may be literal, Jesus' descriptions of Hell in his parables are, by definition, figurative and illustrative, not definitive.

Indeed, even the most conservative Bible dictionaries admit that the word used for Hell (*Gehenna*) was an actual garbage dump just outside of Jerusalem at the Valley of Hinnom. The conservative 1915 *International Standard Bible Encyclopedia* reports that Gehenna is "a transliteration from the Aramaic form of the Hebrew *ge-hinnom* ...," a literal "topographical" location where "the city's offal was collected ... [thus] synonymous with extreme defilement. It has been in turn identified with the depression on the western and southern side of Jerusalem."[110] In short, Gehenna was a trash pit at the edge of town.

The Book of Revelation also speaks in detail of a "lake of fire," but if ever a book were symbolical and metaphorical, it is that of John the Revelator.

No, taken as a whole, **the New Testament *rejects* a Punitive Legalism**, instead sending the message that God has decided on Spirit and Love, not stone and vengeance ... on Forgiveness and

Grace, not Punishment and Law.

Madder than Hell?

Jesus' story of the Prodigal Son has been misconstrued by some as a lesson on the importance of "repentance of sinners." You can find the whole story in Luke 15:11–32. After years of profligate living, the rebellious son finally "came to his senses" and returned to his father (the earthly dad being a symbol of the Father-God). However, if you examine the parable closely, you'll notice **two striking things.**

First: When the son returned to his father, the father did not chide or punish him for his riotous, immoral partying. No, instead, Daddy immediately embraced and welcomed the lad back into the family, no strings attached. He even restored the son's inheritance (by placing the Signet Ring on his finger), despite the fact the boy had already tapped his "trust fund" to buy rounds of drinks for his friends!

Second: The other, older son's anger and jealousy (over the father's no-strings-attached redemption) is condemned more strongly by Jesus than the "riotous living" of the first son. Sometimes the eager vehemence with which pulpit-pounding preachers consign "sinners to hellfire" seems more like jealousy than justice. "I've been a loyal goody-two-shoes ... but my brother, the whoremonger, stumbles back into town ... and you throw a party! It's not fair."

Religious pharisees who are more concerned with "fairness" than with love and forgiveness are the kind that get madder than hell (pun intended) at "soft" Christians such as Mother Teresa, who believed in Universalism and unlimited grace, or at Pastor Rob Bell for suggesting in his book, *Love Wins*, that maybe, just maybe, God won't leave people writhing in fire for all of eternity.[111]

The Radical Story of the Prodigal Son

So, let's revisit the story of the Prodigal Son. What follows is purportedly a true story, although I've lost the original source. I'll tell it as I heard it, devoid of inclusive language:

A Christian missionary to China preached about the Prodigal Son parable to a small congregation new to the faith. After the service, one Chinese man came forward to say that the story had really intrigued him. "I'm an artist," he said, "So I would like to paint a picture from the Parable and give it to the church."

The missionary encouraged him. In a few weeks, the artist returned with an oil painting of the prodigal son coming down the road to home. In the distance, the artist had painted the father with arms crossed, standing by the house, glaring an expression of stern anger.

The missionary tried to explain gently, "You paint very well, but to be honest, you have missed the point of the story. Our God is a *forgiving* God. The father is delighted ... he doesn't even wait for the son to express regret. He *runs* to meet the repentant son. Our Father-God is eager to love and happy to forgive."

"Oh, let me try again." After re-reading the story, the artist understood. In a few weeks, he returned with a second painting. Similar to the first, but this time the father was running down the road toward his son, arms outstretched, smiling.

"Yes, you've really captured the essence of a forgiving God," the missionary exclaimed. Then the pastor paused. "Oh, but it seems you made a mistake. The father is wearing mismatched shoes ... one is red and the other is black."

"I know," the artist replied. "You see, God was in such a hurry to save his lost child that he just grabbed the first two shoes he could find. He didn't care if they matched. He just wanted to be quick to forgive."

God's Shoes Don't Match

I like that image: a God whose shoes don't match. The Gospels "paint" a God with little concern for appearances, whose number one aim is to reach the lost and hurting, to retrieve them, to forgive them, to love them, to embrace them and celebrate their return. This God doesn't care if he gets caught in his bathrobe ... or with bloody sandals. God, as manifest in Jesus, did not hesitate to be seen as a baby born alongside barn manure, as a comic character riding a baby donkey, or being spat upon and beaten to a pulp by whips.[112] All he cares about is you. God is portrayed in the New Testament as the relentless finder of lost souls, the shepherd who climbs into the pit where we have fallen, the loving parent who waits by the window watching ... and then jogs down the road to meet us. Any of us and all of us. The "bad" brother and the "jealous" brother. All are welcomed in. Our God is a God whose shoes may be mottled ... but whose heart-blood runs pure and red.

The Greek word for *All* means EVERYONE

The Apostle Paul wrote unequivocally that when Jesus died on the cross, it was for ALL people. He wrote in Colossians: "For God was pleased to have all his fullness dwell in [Jesus Christ], and through him to reconcile to himself all things, whether things on earth or things in heaven, by making peace through his blood, shed on the cross." The CEV Version renders it this way: "... so that all beings in heaven and on earth would be brought back to God."[113] The Greek word used here for *reconcile* (*apokatallaxai*) is emphatic: "absolutely and totally reconciled." The result is a peaceful, intimate relationship with God (the opposite of being in trouble with a vengeful god). Furthermore, the phrase "all things" (*panta*) means "every person on heaven and earth." In fact, it is this same Greek word that is used in Romans 14:10: "For we will **all** (*panta*) stand before God's judgment seat." The implication is that the same "all" who stand before the throne of judgment will also be the "all" who are reconciled — made right — with God.

Why are conservative Bible literalists so quick to deem a universal reconciliation as **heresy**? The Bible repeatedly teaches that God has a plan for Grace and Love to triumph universally. Paul wrote that "... every knee will bow, every tongue will acknowledge God ..."[114] Even in the Old Testament, we read this in Isaiah 25:8: God "will swallow up death forever. The Sovereign Lord will wipe away the tears from all faces; he will remove his people's disgrace from all the earth." Here again, in this passage promising an escape from death and sorrow, the word "all" (used repeatedly, in fact), in the original Hebrew (*kol*) means "each and everyone." No exceptions.

The Contrary Argument, Examined

Am I cherry picking the verses that support the notion that God will find a way to bring **all** people out of the gates of Sheol? Perhaps. So, consider more verses. In the Epistle to Titus, we find "God has shown us undeserved grace by coming to save **all** people."[115] And Jesus spoke of being lifted up on a crucifixion cross, saying, "And I, when I am lifted up from the earth, will draw **all** people to myself."[116] Again, the "all" that I emphasize here is the same word cited earlier: *panta*. Everyone.

I am not ignoring verses that seem to state the opposite. Let's examine them now. In the New Testament, one of the few Scriptures that raises the possibility of an eternal, hellish punishment is found in 2nd Thessalonians, where it warns that God will bring "... flaming fire, inflicting vengeance on those who do not know God and on those who do not obey ... These will suffer the punishment of eternal destruction ..."[117] Even without claiming this is merely rhetorical, "poetic preaching language," can this really be taken as a specific, literal, theological doctrine of eternal destruction? Think about it objectively. How can there be such a thing as "everlasting destruction"? **Something is either destroyed, or not.** It makes little sense to think of a fire that destroys something, yet that thing (or person) never burns up, is never actually destroyed even through an eternity of burning. As nearly the entire New Testament emphasizes the unlimited forgiveness and inclusiveness of God's love and grace, the few that speak of "everlasting destruction" are the inconsistency. So, the anomalies (like this verse in Thessalonians) must be taken as either figurative/metaphorical language, or as a misunderstanding. Some Bible scholars go even further to say that the phrase "everlasting destruction" is an outright mistranslation — a gross mistake. If you are interested in reading more of about the misuse or misunderstanding of *aion*, the Greek word behind "everlasting destruction," you can start with a few websites I've posted in this Endnote.[118]

Widely-respected and scholarly, Bible commentator William Barclay wrote: "To take the word *aionios*, when it refers to blessings and punishment, to mean lasting forever is to oversimplify, and indeed to misunderstand, the word altogether. It means far more than that. God's nature and character ... [is that of] holy love."[119] In today's context, the late Professor Barclay is considered a mainstream, conservative theologian.

What Did Jesus Say?

Whenever I find a contradiction (here referring to *God as Torturer vs. God as Redeemer*), I turn to Jesus' words for clarity. The one occasion where Jesus clearly spoke of something resembling Hell — as a place in the afterlife of fire and punishment — is found in Luke 16:22–31. Read it. This does **not** seem intended as a literal, textbook description of Hell; it is an illustrative parable, using the common rhetorical tool of Jewish hyperbole (including a touch of humor). Does anyone really think Jesus was telling us, literally, that folks in hellfire could be able to glance up to heaven and chitchat with Abraham, to ask for a drop of water on the tongue? In this anecdote, Jesus even portrays Abraham as playfully yelling back with the equivalent of a modern, humorous taunt: *I wouldn't give you the sweat off my brow if you were dying* *in the desert!* (Not far from the actual wording in verses 24–29). No, the point of the story is to condemn the greed of the self-righteous Pharisees, with an added "bonus point" in an allusion about Jesus' death and resurrection: "cross over," (verse 26) and "rises from the dead," (verse 31).

The English word "Hell" did not even exist until centuries later. Four hundred years after Christ, Jerome translated the Greek into Latin (the "Vulgate" translation), and added the word *Hades* (English = Hell) more than *twice* as many times as it is found in respected Protestant Bible translations (the King James, the American Standard, the New Revised Standard, or the New International Versions). There is nothing near a consensus, even amongst the best translators, as to the exact meaning, or number of times, words now translated "Hell" may have appeared in original manuscripts. A few pages back, we examined the word *Gehenna*, the garbage dump. The Hebrew word *Sheol* and the Greek word *Hades* are, in most verses, more accurately translated as "the place of the dead," not a fiery torture chamber. Indeed, Peter states that God delivered Jesus from "Hades" (the literal Greek used for "place of the dead" in Acts 2:21–32) via the Resurrection. Yet after the resurrection, Jesus had scars from the crucifixion ... but no burns and no ashes on his white robe! Why? Because metaphors don't actually burn things.

With all that said, let's return to the "Hades" parable from Jesus in Luke 16. The word translated "torment" in verse 23, *basanos* (βάσανος), means "to test (metals) by the touchstone, which is a black siliceous stone used to test the purity of gold or silver by the color of the streak produced on it by rubbing it with either metal."[120] The connection of the word to metallurgy is consistent with the concept of the Refiner's Fire — which is consistently the better understanding of any post-mortem, remedial "Hell."

The Refiner's Fire

We can't deny there remains a biblical warning of fire. So, what makes more sense regarding the several phrases in the Bible descriptions of a punishment of fire? According to the Old Testament, descriptions of fires that are God's making are almost always a metaphor of a **refiner's fire**. The object of a refiner's fire is constructive, not destructive. The refiner's fire aims to purify by removing the imperfections, the dross, thus leaving a pure treasure, such as gold, that never rusts or fades. God's plan is to purify humanity from evil and redeem and reconcile with love.

So, biblically speaking, the only consistent way to understand a painful "fire" is in terms of remedial "punishment" intended at improvement, not vengeful spite. I didn't invent this concept of remediation. The Bible teaches it. The final book of the Old Testament, Malachi, prepares the way for the New Covenant by describing the "Day of Reconciliation" this way: "'The messenger of the covenant … will come,' says the Lord Almighty. 'But who can endure the day of his coming? Who can stand when he appears? For he will be like a refiner's fire or a launderer's soap. He will sit as a refiner and purifier of silver; he will purify the Levites and refine them like gold and silver.'"[121]

The New Testament ends with another reference to a refining fire in the afterlife, in the Book of Revelation. But here again, as with Luke 16, it speaks of hell-like punishment using the Greek word *basanos*, which connotes metal testing and refining. 1st Corinthians 3:15 also apparently refers to the redemptive work of a refiner's fire; the Literal Greek says that while a person's material/earthly efforts will be burned away, their eternal spirit "shall be saved … as through fire." If "Hell" is a process of burning away the evil and selfish aspects of our Egos, that process would be, by necessity, painful. Ego surrender is a painful thing … but a good and healthy thing. And for those who resist the process, I can see how it could be a long and agonizing ordeal. (Incidentally, in Revelation 20:10 we find the only clear reference to a torture that lasts "forever and ever," and it refers to *Satan* ... not humans. So, if you insist upon taking that passage literally, perhaps Satan just stubbornly refuses to ever allow God to "refine" him?) We must remember that the vision of Revelation is highly symbolic.

More Scriptures to consider: Paul's First Epistle to Timothy states that God "desires everyone to be saved and to come to the knowledge of the truth."[122] An omnipotent God surely can find a way to save **everyone**. After all, Jesus said that "the gates of Hades will not prevail against" the church (the people of God).[123] 1st Peter 3:19–20 adds this interesting note, indicating that Jesus saved even those already consigned to Sheol: after Jesus' death on the cross, "he went and made proclamation to the imprisoned spirits — to those who were disobedient long ago ..." Note that this does *not* say Jesus only retrieved the *faithful* saints of the Old Testament from Hades. He also freed "those who were disobedient."

A Postscript

The atheist's response to the idea of everlasting punishment is to deny any notion of God, and thus any hope of an Afterlife of *any* sort. This chapter on Hell deserves a postscript about Heaven: the potential for eternal life is clearly affirmed by Scripture (and suggested by several findings in quantum science).[124] The contrast is striking: Scriptures referencing Hell are few, brief and metaphorical; the specific promise of eternal life is made or referenced frequently — in nearly one of every three pages of the New Testament. The teachings by Jesus and the New Testament writers go into great detail about a life beyond this physical one. Here I become a Literalist, and with good reason. The clear promises of a life beyond this world cannot be dismissed, unless a person wishes to throw out the entire Bible as a fairy tale. Personally, I've never read a fairy tale as compelling and as rooted in real, historical personages. Shortly after the events of the New Testament transpired, hundreds of believers — many of whom had met Jesus or the Apostles in person — were willing to die as martyrs rather than to deny the truth they had heard and/ or witnessed.

Quantum science has not proven there is an Afterlife, but it has shown that "spiritual concepts" (unseen worlds, consciousness and connections that seem to last beyond empirical boundaries) are not as crazy as secular scientists once suggested. Most of the major quantum physicists, in my limited study, seem to believe in a God (or a reasonable facsimile), and in the notion of a spiritual realm that goes beyond mechanistic time and space.

Someday we may find that Heaven operates utilizing the same quanta that makes our world go 'round.

Questions for Thought, Study and Group Discussion

If willing, share when you first heard about Hell, or when you first (as a child?) were taught details of fiery, eternal punishment. Can you remember your emotions and thoughts regarding that?

Is it possible for a parent to spare a child from ever experiencing pain? That may seem like a rhetorical question ... so please answer beyond just a "No," and discuss your thoughts on the connection between pain, learning and growth.

Paradox 8
Our Loving God painfully refines our imperfections.

Reflective Quote for Chapter 8
You are in error because you do not know the Scriptures or the power of God.
~ *Jesus, in Matthew 22:29*

Chapter 9

The Paradox of Science χ Religion

Both religion and science require a belief in God. For believers, God is in the beginning, and for physicists He is at the end of all considerations ...
~ *Max Planck, physicist and pioneer of Quantum Theory*

A refusal to use our intelligence honestly is an act of contempt for [God,] who gave us that intelligence.
~ *Ernest Walton, Nobel Prize-winning physicist, and a Christian*

Science and Religion both seek Truth. They have different starting and end points, but need not be enemies. And it should be said that in the long history of Science, it has been guilty of arrogance and ignorance as often as Religion has. As comedian Steve Martin reminded us with his "Theodoric of York" satire of ignorant "barber-doctors," prior to the twentieth century, medical "science" killed more folks than it healed. Robert Boyle and the seventeenth-century founders of modern chemistry discredited medieval alchemy; Quantum physics has shown just how limited seventeenth-century Newtonian physics was. Much of what Darwin wrote in the nineteenth century about Evolution and Natural Selection is being challenged in the twenty-first century by discoveries in molecular biology and genetics (see Endnotes for more on that).[125]

But I am not "anti-Science." My genius older brother is a physics professor, and when we were children, his influence fostered my love of science. If I had his brain for mathematics, I might have become a scientist as well as a minister. So, we grieve when Religion and Science can't also be "brothers."

Religion's Embarrassing Moments

The so-called "War" between Religion and Science has been overstated. Nevertheless, other than the horrible years of the Inquisition, most of the egg on the face of the Church has come from its battles against scientific knowledge — when church leaders stuck stubbornly to a defense of the Bible as Literal and Inerrant. What's worse, often that stubbornness resulted in some very un-Christian behavior. In the 1600s, the Roman Catholic Church placed Galileo under house arrest and banned his book because of his "heretical" view that the earth revolves around the sun. Galileo had tried to convince the authorities to view the solar system through his telescope, so that they might see the truth of his cosmology with their own eyes. According to Galileo, they refused.[126] That blindness to truth, that embrace of ignorance, has haunted religion's reputation ever since.

Some Perspective

It is not helpful to exaggerate the occasional conflicts between religion and science. Currently, we are not at war. Yes, a few outliers are openly hostile, like Rev. Jerry Falwell at one extreme, calling science a lie, and Dr. Sam Harris, at the other. Harris, a prominent atheist, has written that "science must destroy religion," and said that "raising our children to believe" in faith is a "ludicrous obscenity."[127] And sure, tensions will always persist between the two fields, because a spiritual approach is wholly different from the Scientific Method.

But give religion its due: Through most of history, religious institutions have fostered and preserved literature, scientific knowledge and academic advancement. Many of the best colleges in America were founded by churches and churchmen, including Harvard, Yale, Princeton and Emory. The ranks of scientists and academics are filled with clergy, the children of clergy, and devout church-folk. Many great pioneers in science were also people of faith, such as Isaac Newton, who considered himself a theologian as much as a scientist. Newton studied and wrote extensively about the Bible and Christianity (albeit, not always in orthodox ways). Science historians regard James Maxwell as a father of quantum physics, with his foundational work in electromagnetism, wave theory, optics and more. Maxwell was an evangelical Christian and an Elder in the Church of Scotland. Modern genetic studies began with the work of a Catholic monk, Gregor Johann Mendel. Even Charles Darwin attended Christian colleges and studied to become an Anglican clergyman before later pursuing science as a career.

Gary Ferngren, a respected Historian of Science, wrote: "Although popular images of controversy continue to exemplify the supposed hostility of Christianity to new scientific theories, studies have shown that Christianity has often nurtured and encouraged scientific endeavor."[128] Ferngren cites the highly visible cases of when religion fought against science as anomalies; he names Galileo's persecution, various book burnings, and the Scopes "Monkey" Trial as "the exception, not the rule." Across millennia, monastic communities and Church-funded libraries have *preserved* more books than have ever been burned by Christian extremists.

Faith Seeking Understanding?

While the Church (especially the monastic centers) helped preserve culture and knowledge through the Dark Ages, the Church also fought against science. The debate and dialogue between Faith and Reason came early and often in the story of civilization. More than one of the Early Church Fathers tried to merge the two, with mottos such as "faith seeking understanding" (*Fides quaerens intellectum*).[129] But other Christian leaders looked with suspicion at science and intellectual reasoning. For centuries, the Roman Catholic Church tried to violently silence the scholars and heretical scientists. The Vatican threatened Galileo with jail simply for suggesting the Earth revolves around the Sun. Other scientists were tortured and killed.

Religious authority began to erode with the Renaissance and the Enlightenment, and then with the rise of the modern scientific method in the eighteenth and nineteenth centuries, the Christian monopoly was shattered. The Church did not relent. Modernity has been a period of continued *Faith v. Reason* conflict. The end result has been that the Church came out looking very foolish in that struggle, because:

a) The Church, not Science, *started* the "war," and

b) For centuries, the Church (Catholics, Eastern Orthodox and Protestants) refused to face the truth of the scientific method. Church leaders attacked not just the facts, but also demonized the scientists with *ad hominem* insults. The fallout from that war is a continued loss of credibility. Organized religion is losing credibility with much of Western Civilization. Church leaders have, for too long, relied on **fear** to keep the flock inside the corral.

Post-Modernity should Be Post-Fear

As Christians, we need to get past the fear of science in order to make our faith credible for our children and grandchildren. I understand the "anti-intellectualism" or hesitancy among many believers. Scientists are not saints; some are even frauds. Science has its own credibility problems, often slow to change old dogma as new theories emerge and new proofs are applied. Science has its own sins of hubris, its own version of *Scribes and Pharisees*. I'm still mad at medical science for making me feel guilty about eating "unhealthy" eggs for breakfast. For decades, the scientists told us matter-of-factly that eggs caused heart disease. They were insistent, even arrogant ... and wrong. Turns out that eating eggs is not the least bit harmful to one's longevity or heart health![130]

With all that said, the future belongs to those with open

minds, who can reconcile Science and Faith. As mentioned in my *Preface*, I'm aware that Scripture gives ample warnings against trusting human smarts over Godly wisdom. I get that. But human brains are godly gifts. And sometimes facts are facts.

So, we can no longer run from science, fearing it might poison religious truth. Fear is no friend to truth. God is not afraid of our science or our questions. The firm foundations of our faith are **not** based on the literal Genesis creation story (see prior chapters), but rather in far more important things, like the nature of God in Christ, the meaning of love, the transcendence of the spirit. Science can never shake those foundations, nor can science assess or measure faith foundations using statistics or lab-work. If one's faith crumbles because of a physics or biology class, it was an insubstantial faith.

Some denominations (such as the Lutheran-Missouri Synod and the Southern Baptists) and groups (the "Young Earth" Creationists) would have you believe that Orthodoxy has always supported what they see as the literal account of Creation in Genesis. Wrong. Until the Middle Ages, many of the key leaders of Christendom had no problem understanding the Creation story in Genesis as an allegory or metaphor. Saint Augustine of Hippo, one of the early pillars of orthodoxy, had no hesitancy to incorporate secular science into his faith. In his book, *On Christian Doctrine*, he encouraged the application of "worldly" scientific thinking when interpreting Scripture. Augustine was unafraid to allow "pagan" tools, such as rhetoric, logic, history, and the natural sciences, to shed light on Scripture and to expand our knowledge.

Scientists and Religion

People of science have no need to apologize for their faith beliefs, either. Below is a partial list of highly acclaimed physicists who have affirmed **the connection betwixt physics and mysticism/ spirituality**. We could assemble similar lists from all scientific fields.

Niels Bohr: One of the pioneers of atomic energy, Bohr was a spiritual person — despite being unwilling to commit to any single religion. Bohr rejected a purely mechanistic view of reality, and had a strong affinity for mystical Christianity. Speaking of Christian philosopher Soren Kierkegaard, Dr. Bohr said his tome was "one of the most delightful things I have ever read." (As an interesting note regarding Bohr's fondness of Paradox, his personally designed family Coat of Arms features the Ying/Yang symbol of paradox with this motto in Latin: *Contraria sunt complementa*, "opposites are complementary." Thus, I'd like to think he would have enjoyed the book you hold in your hand.)

Albert Einstein: Like many scientists, he viewed institutional religion with suspicion and was troubled by the many apparent contradictions in the Bible. But he did not scoff at the existence of God.

David J. Bohm: A colleague of Einstein and Oppenheimer, this "Renaissance Man" and quantum theory genius also collaborated with the Indian mystic, Jiddu Krishnamurti. His intriguing theories on what he calls "consciousness and the Implicate Order" seem consistent with Dr. Carl Jung's psychological/religious term, the "Collective Consciousness." Bohm's description of a holographic intelligence that is "everything in everything" and a "fundamental ground of all matter" seems consistent with Christian theologian Paul Tillich's concept that "God is the Ground of All Being," which in turn reflects the Book of Acts (17:27): In God "... we live and move and have our being."

Werner Heisenberg: 1932 Nobel Prize Winner in Physics "for the creation of quantum mechanics," Heisenberg refused to be forced into choosing just one side of a dichotomous view of the universe (mechanistic v. metaphysical). In essence, he was saying that choosing an exclusively scientific view or an exclusively religious view would be "a choice between enjoying music or analyzing its structure." We would now call that a "Sophie's Choice." Professor Henry Margenau wrote of him: "Heisenberg ... impressed me by his deep religious conviction. He was a true Christian in every sense of that word."[131]

Fritjof Capra: Another brilliant PhD in theoretical physics, with his best-selling 1975 book, *The Tao of Physics*, Capra was one of the first to awaken popular culture to the fact that modern physics is bridging the gap between empirical science and the mystical realms. Subtitled "An Exploration of the Parallels between Modern Physics and Eastern Mysticism," in it he writes: "Science does not need mysticism and mysticism does not need science, but man needs both." Heisenberg befriended Capra, finding Capra's book a helpful way to view quantum discoveries.

Don Page: Dr. Page works in quantum cosmology and theoretical gravitational physics. His studies, including collaborations with the famous Professor and atheist, Stephen Hawking, have not diminished the zeal of his Christian outlook.

Henry Stapp: With a PhD in particle physics, Stapp has a mystical view somewhat akin to Buddhism, and believes a "consciousness" pervades the universe. Dr. Stapp has tried to prove scientifically that the human mind can interact with external matter via quantum processes in the brain ... which in layman's terms, borders on "psychokinesis."

William A. Tiller: Like Stapp, Dr. Tiller claims to have developed empirical evidence proving that conscious thought can alter external reality. With a PhD in physics, he is author of several books that deal with the overlap of physics and metaphysics, including, *Conscious Acts of Creation: The Emergence of a New Physics*.

Stephen M. Barr: Professor of Particle Physics at the University of Delaware, Barr writes from his Christian perspective in his well-reasoned book, *Modern Physics and Ancient Faith*. There he states that the latest breakthroughs in science have "... given us new eyes that allow us to see down to the deeper roots of the world's structure, and there all we see is order and symmetry of pristine mathematical purity." And he attributes that pristine symmetry to the Divine Creator. He argues convincingly (to me, anyway) that believing in God is far more reasonable than believing in a solely materialistic universe.

Ernest Walton: After winning the 1951 Nobel Prize in Physics, he said: "One way to learn the mind of the Creator is to study His creation. We must pay God the compliment of studying His work of art."

A Beautiful, Creative View of the Cosmos

The point here is that many of the best minds of history see the grandeur, complexity and order of the universe and stand in reverential awe. They can envision a quantum God, a mystical Creator bigger than the literal notion of a bearded old man on a throne. Though not a physicist, Immanuel Kant certainly had one of those brilliant and elastic brains; he embraced paradox and rejected a mechanistic view of life. Kant, considered one of the most influential philosophers in history, stated that "belief in a wise and great Author of the world is generated ... by the glorious order, beauty and providential care everywhere displayed in nature."[132]

You may also know the name of Lord William Kelvin, more renown because his name is on the Kelvin temperature scale than for his work in thermodynamics or as originator of the concept of Absolute Zero. A devout Christian, Kelvin stated: "I believe that the more thoroughly science is studied, the further does it take us from anything comparable to atheism." So, to repeat: the same imaginative brains that embrace a quantum universe are usually open to the idea of a quantum God.

God and the Entangled Connection

Spooky Quantum Action (Entanglement) is a physics concept

begging to be included in discussions of science *v.* religion. Not because the word "spooky" might evoke the term "Holy Ghost," aka the Holy Spirit. No, this is more than a mere pun. Spooky Action shows properties we once assigned to magical realms. Quantum entanglement describes two particles so intimately connected that they share one identical quantum state **even when separated**. The "magic" or transcendent part is revealed when scientists take those twin entangled particles and separate them miles apart in space. In layman's terms, one particle always "knows" what the other is doing (e.g., charge and spin), and instantly reflects any changes made in the twin particle, even if the particles are moved a thousand miles away from each other.[133] Some researchers believe this entanglement also transcends Time itself (past, present, future)![134] As I mentioned in the Preface, the cutting edge of science not only seems to be approaching science fiction, it sometimes sounds closer to voodoo![135]

Physicists continue exploring this mysterious connection of quantum entanglement and its relation to "space-time geometry" (how quanta, with their movements and connections, give shape to the universe). John Preskill, Feynman Professor of Theoretical Physics at CIT, asserts that the makeup of all "stuff" in the universe is "not really geometry anymore. It's something else, an emergent thing [that arises] from something more fundamental."[136] With mystics speaking separately about the *Manifest* emerging from the *Unmanifest* (the *seen* Creation that emerges from the *unseen* Creator), it's not a far stretch to say that quantum physics is encroaching on spiritual territory.

The visible (the material world) and the invisible emerge from the *Logos*, the vast, creative-yet-ordered Spirit of God. The gospel of John, using this Greek term, tried to explain the divine mystery: "In the beginning was the *Logos* ... and the *Logos* (Word) **was** God."[137]

Goodbye Lazy Assumptions

In contrast, I wonder if Atheists and Fundamentalists both share the same shortcoming: **a lack of imagination**. Atheists narrowly define the universe with "empirical science," attempting to reduce everything to basic, material facts of science and math formulas. The mystic apologist, Evelyn Underhill, admonishes them: "We must break with our inveterate habit of taking the 'visible world' for granted; our lazy assumption that somehow science is 'real' and metaphysics is not."[138]

Could a "lazy assumption" also be behind the approach of Fundamentalists (Christian and Islamic) who see the world in black 'n white, resting in simple dualities, never going beyond ink on a page, forgetting that Scripture is constrained by the limits of human language? Deeper and broader realities call for an open mind, a willingness to understand metaphors and paradoxes, and a soaring spirit that rises above the concrete, literal approach that is shared, ironically, by both Atheists and Fundamentalists.

Forgive me if this sounds insulting, but my conviction about the matter robs me of softer words.

Questions for Thought, Study and Group Discussion

Why do you think Evolution and Creationism have become such emotional topics?

For most of the people you know (your personal circles), which tends to be the greater authority: Religion, or Science?

At what points and in what ways do you agree with this chapter's assertions? In what ways do you disagree?

Paradox 9

Science and religion approach reality differently, but both desire the same end: to know Truth.

Reflective Quote for Chapter 9

The first gulp from the glass of natural sciences will turn you into an atheist, but at the bottom of the glass God is waiting for you.

~ *Werner Heisenberg, winner of the 1932 Nobel Prize in Physics*

Chapter 10

The Paradox of Orthodoxy: Stone χ Spirit

Christians who try to reconcile every doctrine in a humanly rational way are inevitably drawn to extremes. Seeking to remove all mystery and paradox, they emphasize one truth or aspect of God's Word at the expense of another ...
~ *John MacArthur, Conservative Christian Author and Bible Commentator*

[This is] a new covenant — not of the letter but of the Spirit; for the letter kills, but the Spirit gives life. [This covenant is] written not with ink but with the Spirit of the living God, not on tablets of stone but on tablets of human hearts.
~ *2nd Corinthians 3:6,3, excerpted*

This chapter is admittedly a hodge-podge, a "Miscellany" of related topics touched upon earlier, but still deserving of more explication.

Let me start with explaining what I mean by "Stone χ Spirit." Again, χ means "in paradox with," not an adversarial relationship. Stone is not bad. God created the material, "concrete" world for a reason. God wrote laws in stone for a reason. The barbarians of Moses' day certainly needed the Ten Commandments presented to them in a "solid" and clear manner, and stone did the trick. Then the metaphor extends to any written Law, whether in stone, on scrolls or in books. Laws have their place. Laws set the boundaries for civilization, creating an environment of safety wherein the Spirit can grow.

Spiritual growth is the goal. So in this paradox, Spirit is superior to Stone. The New Testament makes it clear that God's ultimate ideal is **not** an outward, written Law written, but an inward Love written by the Spirit on our hearts. This ideal is found, to a lesser degree, in the Old Testament. Jeremiah 31:31, 33 predicted that, "The days are coming," declares the Lord, "when I will make a new covenant ... I will put my law in their minds and write it on their hearts." That New Covenant became manifest and explicit in the New Testament. Paul referred to this new covenant (agreement) as a "letter from Christ" that is "written not with ink but with the Spirit of the living God, not on tablets of stone but on tablets of human hearts."[139] He also speaks of initiation into the family of God as "of the heart, by the Spirit, not by the written code."[140]

Surrendering Orthodoxy?

This statement from my Preface bears repeating: The Bible is not outdated; our interpretation of it may be. In asking for a surrender of orthodoxy, I'm not suggesting we throw the baby out with the bathwater. Doctrine, creeds and established church teachings can be good things, as long as they don't become so "set in stone" they become false idols that rule over us. **God** should be our authority, our place of trust, more than doctrines. Even when those doctrines are rooted in Scripture, church tradition and experience, doctrines are still HUMAN teachings. Don't make them false, graven idols.

It may be helpful here in this penultimate chapter to restate more of my Preface: Orthodoxy means "correct doctrine, approved opinion, or right teaching," a word assembled from the Greek and Latin root words for "right/straight/correct" and "opinion/teaching." This begs the question of *who* gets to determine *which* doctrine is right/correct. Most "orthodox" teachings are in dispute in one way or another. Within the Christian tradition, some core tenets of orthodoxy have a strong "majority consensus": The Canon of Scripture (39 Old Testament books, 27 New Testament books[141]), the manifestation of God as a Trinity (Creator/Son/Holy Spirit) and the divinity of Christ, the principles of a fallen Creation and a need for Redemption and Grace. But few to none are *unanimously* embraced to the letter. Christendom has more shades of variation than a rainbow. Sacramental ritual, in particular, is hotly debated amongst the various denominations and sects of Christendom.

The Ecumenical Movement, with good intentions, has tried to de-emphasize our differences. And I'm all for unity. Nevertheless, let us not pretend that there is some set, absolute Orthodoxy that *all* Christians embrace. Never has been, never will be.

This means that when anyone condemns another as a heretic, an element of arrogance is unavoidable. We should be most cautious in saying, "I know the truth, and you don't."

Why Literalism and Fundamentalism Persists

I have a dear friend who was a gifted, highly successful Southern Baptist minister. He is still a fine and dedicated pastor … but now serves a non-denominational parish. Why? Because a Baptist congregation in Arkansas saw fit to throw him out of their church for the simple "sin" of reading too many books outside of their narrow theological mindset. As comedian Dave Barry is known to say, "I'm not making this up."

Understandably, people can become uncomfortable with ideas that vary from their childhood rearing. And most folks love simplicity. Fundamentalist religion is attractive to many as it reduces the complexities of life and spirit, of humanity and divinity, to facile platitudes. But that does not explain why those of us who question some of the details of Literalism get met with outright hostility. What is that about?

Without any intent to insult, let's consider that perhaps **Fundamentalism is a psychological issue more than it is a theological** one. Jungian analyst Lyn Cowan offers this definition of *neurosis*: "If we imagine a neurosis to be a one-sided attitude, then neurosis is a false narrowness, like a person with two good eyes who wears blinders. Those things that could widen his vision — the peripheral, the nuances, the new angles — are unseen. A neurosis is not as much blindness as a limited vision whose limitation is not perceived."

Cowan's words were not written to apply to conservative fundamentalists, yet maybe they do. Neurosis is mostly rooted in fear, and here the fear is *Satan*. The very things that could give a fundamentalist a broader, balanced understanding, they dismiss as Satanic. I find that odd, because fundamentalists also express such extreme confidence in the power of God. Why give the Devil so much power? As quoted in Chapter 4, "Fear is the mind-killer." The lack of new perceptions are not just unseen limitations, they are "impossible perceptions," never allowed inside the blinders at all. At times, it goes beyond neurosis. It is a willful and active rejection of even the *thought* of wider vision. (And if by chance, you're a Fundamentalist who has read this far: prove me wrong and be brave enough to continue reading. I am not your enemy.)

The Opposite of Literalism Is not Liberalism

Consider Saint Augustine's warning against adamantly asserting one single "right" interpretation of a Scripture passage: "In matters that are obscure and far beyond our vision, even in such as we may find treated in Holy Scripture, different interpretations are sometimes possible ... In such a case, we should not rush in headlong and so firmly take our stand on one side that, if further progress in the search of truth justly undermines this position, we too fall with it."[142] Unfortunately, his sage advice has not been heeded in American religion.

Somewhere in my home library is an old book of essays by a dozen Conservative Baptist theologians, each making basically the same argument: that the rite of baptism by full immersion (rather than sprinkling water symbolically on the head, or other methods) is the *only* acceptable method of holy baptism and initiation into Christianity. The Baptist authors were all educated, intelligent folk, but so emphatic in their convictions, their arguments were polemical, not deliberative. Their essays spun a variety of rationales, but primarily rested on a literal translation of the Greek word *baptizo*, as found in verses such as Mark 16:16: "He that believes and is baptized shall be saved; but he that does not believe shall be condemned." They asserted — correctly — that the Greek word used in the gospels, *baptizo*, means "to cleanse by dipping in water." Since they had no dry cleaners in biblical times, all methods of washing clearly imply an immersive washing.

However, proving the literal, dictionary meaning of a word does not mean that we can use the word identically across contexts. Consider modern English: a person can be "brainwashed" without removing their cranium and applying soap. In the process of interpretation, Logic must be employed further down the line of application. Could it possibly be that God would condemn millions of believers to Hell simply because they didn't use enough water in their baptism? Can any intelligent, loving person truly believe that?

Those Baptist scholars were not wrong in their Greek-to-English transliteration. The problem lies in their proposition that we can only apply Scripture in a strictly literal form. Rejecting the figurative nature of religious language, and ignoring the symbolic nature of baptism as a *ritual*, they instead applied an inflexible, universal application: "Baptism must be, can *only* be, done by submersing one's entire body in water." Yes, some (not all) of those Baptist scholars actually asserted that immersion baptism is crucial for eternal salvation! Their adherence to literalism and legalism results in a heresy: that God is a petty scribe who would doom a person to never-ending, fiery torture just because there wasn't enough water splashed on them in baptism.

An Achilles Heel

Can we not see the absurdity of their proposition, even without a Greek word study? What if I were to descend into a baptismal pool, but my underwear waistband's tag prevented the "holy water" from reaching a square centimeter of my skin? Apparently, some literalists could assert that I was not "fully immersed," and would thus have me skewered on a rotisserie for all eternity. Ludicrous, you say? Nevertheless, that is exactly where such a narrow matter-of-fact theology takes us. Such belief is more akin to the fairy tales of Greek mythology: legend told that the "god-man" Achilles was as invulnerable as comic-book Superman ... except for his heel. To give him his godlike strength, his mother had dipped (baptized!) him in the magical, mythical waters of the River Styx as an infant, holding him by only his heels. As an adult warrior, he fought without injury, until finally killed by an arrow piercing his unbaptized heel ... thus the term "Achilles heel."

Should we be using "holy water" as if it were mythic magic, like water from the River Styx? A dogmatic definition of baptism as *water immersion* assigns the power of salvation to the magical water itself, rather than understanding that the water merely symbolizes the true spiritual power of God. *God* is doing the cleansing and saving and initiating. Not the water. True spirituality is not fairy tale magic.

Why We Should Use a Blowtorch for Baptizing

To illustrate the farcicality of such non-contextual, non-figurative application of Scripture, I will apply the exact same reasoning employed by the Literalists in demanding immersive water-baptism ... this time to Scripturally prove that baptism should be done by FIRE:

In Luke 3:16–17, "John answered, saying to all, 'I indeed baptize you with water; but One mightier than I is coming ... He [Jesus] will baptize you with the Holy Spirit and fire." Yep, he said **fire**.

The Greek word which John the Baptist used here is *pyri*, which means a very hot, burning fire. From *pyri* comes our English word, *pyre* — as in a funeral pyre.

Since Jesus is our model and, according to the literal gospel, was baptizing using fire, therefore we should use a flame thrower at every church to cleanse and purify new converts with a quick inferno.

This New Testament teaching is consistent with the Old Testament, which frequently speaks of God's people being cleansed or refined "by fire" (see Zachariah 13:9; Psalm 66:10; Isaiah 6:6 7). Several Old Testament references are to the "refiner's fire," which means flames hot enough to melt metal. Any wimpy substitution of a small ceremonial candle would be the equivalent of milquetoast Anglicans using sprinkling as a substitute for a full immersion.

And finally, the use of fire for Holy Spirit baptism is found in the practice of the Early Church: "They saw what seemed to be tongues of fire that ... came to rest on each of them. All of them were filled with the Holy Spirit ..."[143]

So, if the Baptists wish to be consistent with their literalistic approach to biblical interpretation, they MUST begin to burn people as part of the baptismal rite!

Before critics dismiss my hopefully humorous satire as absurdist, please tell me what is different about my **flame-thrower** literalism vs. **immersion baptism** literalism? Who really is the absurdist here?

Incidentally, as a pastor serving near the coast, I had the honor of preaching summers at the Gulf State Park. There I baptized more than a few folks by immersion in the Gulf of Mexico; in my church, I also employed the methods of sprinkling and pouring. I've not observed any difference in the outcome!

1st Peter 3:21 makes it clear, saying "… this water symbolizes baptism …" Thayer's Greek Lexicon tells us that Peter's word "symbolize," *antitupon*, means "representative; a thing resembling another." A symbol or metaphor. So, the Bible matter-of-factly states that baptismal water is a *metaphor* ... just as baptizing with fire was clearly intended as a metaphor. This point is inarguable. Yet, how can so many, who claim strict devotion to the truth of the Bible, get the truth of the Bible so wrong? Yes, I'm being arrogant. But they are still wrong.

Angels Dancing on the Head of a Pin

Religion does seem to prompt people to debate minutiae. In the seventeenth century, William Chillingworth reported that unnamed scholastics had debated "whether a Million Angels may not fit upon a needle's point." Even the wise Thomas Aquinas had pondered if "several angels," being ethereal, could "be in the same place" simultaneously. (Answer: in quantum physics, they might!)

Two co-workers from different denominations were talking about their different perspectives on faith, and one explained that even within his denomination, there had been a split over a minor point of doctrine: "One group believes in a pre-Tribulation Rapture, and the other in a post-Tribulation Rapture," he explained. "There have been heated arguments over the issue for as long as anyone can remember. But I feel sure my side is correct on this issue." Whereupon his friend inquired, "Which does your group believe in ... the pre-Tribulation or the post-Tribulation?" The first man paused, then replied, "For the life of me, I can't remember."

Entire books have been written, strongly defending each position, despite the fact that the Bible is not the least bit clear or unequivocal in supporting either view.

Elephants in the Dark

Truth is like the oft-repeated Sufi fable of the elephant in the dark. One man grasped the elephant's leg, and tried to define the giant mammal as "a big pillar." Another held his tail, and declared, "This animal is like a rope." And a third man grasped its writhing trunk and announced, "This beast is a form of serpent." They were all partly right, but failed at understanding the total truth about the animal until daybreak. We all face the grand temptation to think we have THE answer. But if humility were a voice, it would tell us otherwise. We have missed a big part of the truth by **being too insistent about our piece of the elephant in the dark.**

To extend the metaphor, one man thinks the truth is alive and changeable (the writhing trunk), and another thinks the elephant of truth is solid and eternally set in stone (the pillar-sized leg). Both are true, but they **can *only* be true when part of the same** beast ... that is, when held together in the living "animal" called *paradox*. Let's illustrate these abstracts: the pantheistic ultra-liberal says "there is no absolute truth," (or "God is dead" or "all religions are the same"), while the religious fundamentalist obstinately insists that there is only One God and One Literal Word of God (or "the Bible said it, that settles it"). Are they both right, both wrong, or both touching a piece of the same elephant? Truth may be like a mountain: it's always there, in a daily, practical sense very permanent, un-moveable and solid ... and yet, from a quantum-physics viewpoint, the mountain is undergoing constant change and motion. Rock consists of speeding protons, neutrons, electrons and quarks, and the entire mountain is never at rest, hurtling through space as the globe spins, even as the Earth orbits the sun at a speed of 67,000 miles per hour![144]

A Crucial Controversy of Our Day: Sex

To some, these matters may seem abstract or irrelevant to our daily lives. Nothing could be more timely, though, than the issue of SEX. And our view of religion is directly tied to our political views and our social struggle with issues of gender choice, sexual mores, equal rights, treatment of women — the daily headlines. We have already broached the issue of sexuality, including a consideration of what sort of intimate metaphor we use in describing God's gender. I hope we can at least agree on this fact: most religions recognize the complementary differences between female and male, yet seek a unity in God. Even the "male-dominated" Christian faith quotes the Apostle Paul: "There is neither Jew nor Gentile, neither slave nor free, nor is there male and female, for you are all one in Christ Jesus" (Galatians 3:28).

Let's now dive further into the controversy of sexuality and religion.

Gender Confusion

When it comes to sexuality, I'm a traditional male raised with Southern sensibilities. But I am stunned at the level of animosity toward gays exhibited by some Christians, and at the vitriol and confusion surrounding the topic of homosexuality.

The messy dilemma for the Church is, "How can we be true to literal Scripture (which presents heterosexual marriage as the ideal) and be true to a gospel that calls for love and acceptance/inclusion?" Extreme Fundamentalists just say (literally) "to hell with it." As in, "Gays: go directly to Hell, do not pass *Go*, do not collect $200." Extreme Liberals (e.g., Unitarians, the "Jesus Seminar," *et al.*) simply disregard Scriptures that do not fit their rubric. That approach then begs the question of how we can consistently view Scripture as authoritative and trustworthy. Why even associate oneself with the Christian faith if you view Scripture as irrelevant and untrustworthy? This is where the extremes are so polarized, they are no longer in a paradox, they are in a war. It's not that this author is "in the middle." I have no interest in being in the war at all. Let's consider alternatives.

The Middle Is Not the Answer

Some well-meaning Christian moderates attempt to find a middle ground. This is an illusion. You cannot stand in the middle of a battleground without being shot.

In seeking a different approach, we must understand that most homosexuals are not satisfied with mainstream denominations' parsing — that it might be okay to be homosexual as long as you aren't a "practicing homosexual." Nor are they happy with grudging, false claims of inclusion, like: "We love the sinner but hate the sin ... you gays can be part of our congregation, because we LOVE you ... but just don't rock the boat." Asking homosexuals to participate in a "Don't ask, don't tell" charade is asking for people to live a lie. I am an ordained United Methodist minister, but I am no longer comfortable with my denomination's wishy-washy stance that makes gays second-class citizens. The United Methodist position has more to do with ecclesiastical politics and fear than with seeking truth.

A Way Forward?

So how do we preserve an appropriate respect for Scripture *and* a love for all humans? Embracing paradox is a start. Churches could say: "We embrace *both*: we embrace Scripture as God's holy word (albeit mediated through flawed human language), AND we fully embrace you regardless of who you are married to ... and we shall continue, whether liberal, conservative or in-between, to struggle to find out what the emerging context means for us as people of faith." This is not a mamby-pamby "Don't ask, don't tell," not a sweeping under the carpet, but instead, an humble acceptance of the fact that **we don't have all the answers.** Even Conservatives should be willing to err on the side of love and humility. And for homosexuals, participating in church unity must include a willingness to allow other Christians to honestly struggle with the issue, even if feels like they are not being 101 percent accepted.

With so much fear and insecurity on both sides of this debate, I doubt we'll see a quick resolution. Jesus' warning to institutionalized religion against trying to put "new wine in old wineskins"[145] seems apropos, so my advice to the "Establishment" (the entrenched denominational leaders): *If you don't risk stretching, you may become a dead, discarded old wineskin.*

A Christian Columnist Speaks Hard Truth

Syndicated OpEd Columnist Leonard Pitts wrote these challenging words:

One of the more vexing failings of modern Christianity: its inability to get there on time … [O]n issues where it should take the lead, where it should make noise and news, challenging the *status quo* … the great body of Christendom always seems to bring up the rear, arriving decades late … Why is Christianity so often so slow? Maybe it's because there has grown up among us an unfortunate tendency to equate Christianity with conservatism. The effect has been to shrink the Gospel of Christ — a radical compassion that touched prostitutes, lepers, tax collectors, adulterers, women and other third-class citizens of his time — to a narrow and exclusionary faith of narrow and exclusionary concerns: criminalize abortions, demonize gays and that's pretty much it. But you know what? When children are abandoned, hungry or abused … when the poor are exploited … these should be matters of religious conscience, too…. Faith is not an excuse for getting there last. It's an obligation to get there first.[146]

3000-Year-Old Norms Are Slow to Change

While Christ is not an enemy to gays and lesbians, there is nothing in his canonical teachings that endorses the homosexual act. Jesus was enmeshed in Jewish law and patriarchy. Jewish law obviously did not condone homosexuality. On the issue of marriage and sexuality, Jesus re-affirmed the Old Testament concept that God's ideal plan for this life is that a man and a woman marry and "become one flesh." Even the most radical homosexual activist would have to admit that survival of the species has depended, for thousands of years, upon heterosexual procreation. That is, from a biblical perspective, the ideal.

And yet, Christian orthodoxy has taught for centuries that we live in a "fallen" and imperfect world in which the ideal is rarely realized on any topic. I cannot tell the parent of a homosexual that their child is "going to Hell" for being outside the perfect biblical ideal of heterosexual marriage. After all, Jesus himself was outside the "ideal," because he never married! Many of the teachings of Jesus set a standard of perfection for which I strive, but rarely attain. Flawed as I am, how could Jesus send me to everlasting torture when my best intent is to fulfill his two great commandments to love God and to love neighbor?

Jesus' Pragmatic Approach to Sexuality

Consider this case when Jesus encountered a woman, perhaps a prostitute, who had clearly violated the letter and the spirit of Jewish law of fidelity in marriage. The "religious" folk were about to pelt the adulteress with stones until a painful death. Jesus interrupted the stoning with his famous statement, "Let those without sin cast the first stone." He saved the woman's life, and then instructed her to "go and sin no more."

Homosexuals may object to this analogy, maintaining they are not sinning. But hear me out. In the case of the adulteress woman, Jesus did not use the occasion to endorse promiscuity or to challenge the spirit of the Jewish law. Fidelity in sex makes for stable marriages, eliminates sexually transmitted diseases, and provides an intimate bonding between spouses, among other benefits to society. We can also understand the prohibitions against homosexuality in Old Testament times, when the "tribe" valued reproduction as a way to preserve population numbers in dangerous, precarious times. To homosexual promiscuity in Bible times, Jesus might have also said, "Go and sin no more."

But we honestly do not know what Jesus would say in **our** time and culture — except that it would be loving. We can't prove it based on Scripture, but I strongly suspect Jesus would bless homosexual marriage and fidelity. What we do know is that Jesus never condemned homosexuals to Hell. Never.

What Jesus *did* condemn is the hard-nosed, judgmental, murderous attitude of the Pharisees. While Jesus never embraced homosexuality as an ideal, his tolerant and forgiving attitude on so many other topics ran counter to much of the legalistic and extremist practices (and punishments) of the religious leaders of his day. Were a homosexual being stoned, Jesus would step in and stop it. It is also fair to say that the teachings of Jesus support gay rights, as a political expression of his ethic of love, justice and equality. It would not be fair to the historical record to say that he would recommend homosexuality as an ideal lifestyle. But without a doubt, Jesus would be [is!] horrified at the current hate-crimes against gays.

With all that said, we must now ask: Why do so many modern Christians shrug off the various sexual sins of the Bible patriarchs (polygamists and philanderers like Abraham, Samson, David, Solomon, etc.), yet they go into hysterics over the idea of two same-gendered people sharing wedding vows in the church building? David the Adulterer danced naked in the Temple; yet, fully clothed, fully committed, sexually-faithful same-gender couples are prohibited from holding their marriage ceremony in most Christian churches.

Understanding Paul

While Jesus did speak a few times about the value of "male and female" becoming "one" in marriage, he gave no explicit prohibition of homosexual marriage. So, defenders of "Traditional Marriage" (which didn't even exist during most of Bible times) turn to the words of Paul. Yet this must be said: the *initial* and *primary* purpose of Paul's epistles was *not* to serve as a timeless, universal message. An epistle is not a book, it is a **letter**. Each of them were specific handwritten notes ... personal and somewhat informal, including salutations that addressed Paul's church friends by name. If we translated Paul's letter to the church in Corinth into a modern text message, it would be: "btw, Aquila & Priscilla say 'Hi!'"

The epistles do contain timeless messages and guidance about Christianity, and I have no problem with the traditional belief that the New Testament epistles were preserved because they contain divine inspiration; they have a place in the biblical canon. Still, we must admit that the teachings found in the epistles are not as essential and authoritative as the words of Jesus. (Today, churches acknowledge this by having the congregation stand for the reading of the Gospel ... not for the Epistles.)

The churches Paul addressed were not mega-churches; most met in homes, and none met in Joel Osteen-sized stadiums. Paul's circle of early Christian friends likely numbered in scores, not thousands ... a tiny group compared to most Facebook "Friends" lists. The rhetorical style of the apostolic writers is far more thoughtful than the usual "Facebook post"; nevertheless, much of the New Testament is written in an informal, conversational style that more closely resembles social media chat than it does a doctoral dissertation. Paul's *Epistle to the Romans* could be viewed as a thesis paper, but that's an exception, not the rule.

Perhaps Paul had hoped his words would be preserved and passed on to future generations ... but there is little evidence that he thought in those terms. His messages were usually urgent, immediate, intimate prescriptions for people he knew, to help them through the pressing problems of their day. Preachers love to bandy about comparisons between modern America and the "corrupt pagans" of Rome, but truly, the cultures of Asia Minor, Greece and the rest of the Roman Empire of the first century are not at all analogous to our own. We do not have the threat of lions eating us in a gladiatorial contest, nor do we have to deal with temple prostitutes stirring up orgies in our worship services.

The "Lost Gospels" Alternative

An "easy way out" for some believers is to seek alternative moral codes in so-called "Lost Gospels," such as the Gnostic Gospels (e.g., *The Gospel of Thomas*) or other Apocryphal and post-biblical writings. Some gnostic writings are even interpreted to claim that Jesus was either gay, or had an affair with Mary Magdalene. Three problems with those claims: First, the "Gnostic gospels" simply do not have the historical reliability of the four New Testament gospels. Second, the Gnostic gospels so blatantly contradict the canonized gospel, even if we were to accept them as valid, it would only create greater contradictions and inconsistencies. Third, in Jesus' time, if the Jewish leaders felt there was any possibility that Jesus had violated the Jewish prohibitions against sex outside of marriage (either heterosexual or homosexual), they would have surely used this in their case against him. Instead, they simply told the Roman governor, Pilate, that Jesus had broken the Jewish law against *blasphemy* — claiming he was God. Even though Jesus did not protest, the charge did not convince Pilate that the accused was deserving of the death penalty. Pilate even tried to free Christ. At that point, if the Jewish leaders could have claimed additional "sexual crimes," it would have bolstered their case for execution. As a bonus for the leaders, this would have discredited Jesus among the masses. The fact that they made no such claim demonstrates that leaders feared losing all credibility with Jesus' followers, who knew that Jesus had been sexually pure. Jesus never denied other charges against him: that he broke Sabbath laws occasionally, that he claimed special authority as the "Son of God" and his evocation of the divine name "I AM." Jesus could be called a blasphemer, but the historical record shows that Jesus was celibate.

The Mystery of Marriage

The most curious word Jesus gave us on sexuality and marriage was in answer to a question about what marriage would be like in heaven. He said that there, no one would be given in marriage. Mysterious as the Afterlife seems, we can only assume that Paul's later statement is true: in Christ there is no male and female. Some form of spiritual unity and equality will exist in the kingdom of heaven, which shall free us from the tensions and struggles of sex as we now know it. Perhaps in freeing us from the human compulsion to procreate and to seek personal pleasure, God will give us a deeper pleasure and fulfillment than we can imagine. Perhaps when the barriers of this fallen existence are torn down, we shall be overflowing with a spiritual love from our human family (and from God) that shall satisfy us more thoroughly than our biological feeling ever could.

Summary

In sum: Jesus was far more "liberal" regarding sexuality and political rights than most were in the culture of his time. The gospel writers left us with his endorsement of fidelity in marriage and celibacy in singleness, his ambiguity on homosexual marriage, and with a promise that in the ultimate, ideal kingdom of God, sexuality will no longer be an issue.[147] That's right: Jesus left us with a paradox regarding sexuality. What he clearly would *not* have done is blessed the kind of arrogant, judgmental ostracism of gays we see all too often in our time.

Reasonable, civilized Christians do not stone fortune-tellers, nor do we fret over the long list of other minor infractions punishable by death in the Old Testament. Yet at a time when we are realizing that homosexuality is not so much a choice as it seems to be programmed from birth and/or early childhood, we still enforce Old Testament rules against homosexuality, even casting people out of churches and pulpits for this "flaw." The inconsistency is exposed further, as plenty of priests/pastors remain in pulpits and church hierarchies even while guilty of other sins, such as greed or lust for power. Is this fair? When it comes to gender, is the church's intolerant, unforgiving, selective judgment even *Christian*?

This tension between "Stone and Spirit" can no longer be dismissed in favor of legalism and literalism; it is time to quit disparaging those of us who plead for moderation and grace, writing us off as "Liberals" or "Secularists." The question goes to the core of the gospel. How will we define our faith for future generations? If our priority is to focus on nitpicking what the Latin's called "peccadilloes," the tiny sins like playing the lottery, smoking a cigarette, cursing, etc., then we have missed the priorities laid out so clearly by Jesus. Jesus' priorities for us are clear: he gave us the Great Commission (to teach truth and grace to the world) and the Great Commandment (to love God and to love neighbor). And if that wasn't clear enough, Jesus *modeled* it with acts of servanthood: caring for the poor, healing the infirmed, befriending the outcast — even promising eternal life to a criminal.

Baptist evangelist Tony Campola was a darling of evangelical Christian Conservatism … until he said this. Speaking to a Christian audience, Dr. Campola bluntly proclaimed: "I have three things I'd like to say today. First, while you were sleeping last night, 30,000 kids died of starvation or diseases related to malnutrition. Second, most of you don't give a shit. [Pause.] Third … what's worse is that you're more upset with the fact I just said 'shit' than you are that 30,000 kids died last night."[148]

Priorities. If anyone can show me a higher priority than Love, I'm listening.

Questions for Thought, Study and Group Discussion
If you are active in a local congregation, what do you think would have happened if, from the podium, your pastor/rabbi/imam/teacher had said something similar to what Dr. Campola

said (above ... including the word "shit")?

Discuss these extremes: Worldwide, Fundamentalism is growing. Most religions do call for moral purity, and there are signs that many people are longing for structure and order. But our society has become more "loose" and permissive ... the public sphere is now R-rated. Where do you think things are headed, long-term?

Paradox 10

The Word of God is transmitted to us via human language, and received through the filters of our personal time and place ... but the Word is Love.

Reflective Quote for Chapter 10

Intelligent people are always ready to learn. Their ears are open for knowledge.

~ *Proverbs 18:15, NLT*

Chapter 11

The Paradox of God as Knowable χ Unknowable

All matter originates and exists only by virtue of a force which brings the particles of an atom to [vibrate, yet be held together]. [B]ehind this force [is] a conscious and intelligent mind. This mind is the matrix of all matter.
~ *Max Planck, physicist and a pioneer of Quantum Theory*

The whole world, gathered as it were under one ray of the sun, was brought before his eyes.
~ *Gregory the Great, on a vision of Benedict of Nursia*

How does the Finite come to grasp the Infinite? If there is an answer to this question, it too is a paradox. A key aim in religion is to encounter, and come to know, God. Yet most definitions of God include an aspect of mystery. God is by definition ineffable — in one sense, unknowable. The paradox is salient: God is at once too big for us to grasp *and* intimately connected to us.

Most religions teach that the Creator God wants to dwell intimately in us or with us. Christianity speaks at once of Jesus as a *friend*, and as the *Magnum Mysterium*, the vast and unfathomable Spirit. Modern evangelicalism tends to push only one side of the paradox: "A personal relationship with Jesus." In all of human history, I can't identify anyone else I'd rather have as friend, mentor and spiritual teacher than Jesus of Nazareth. But the Gospel of John asks us to broaden our understanding far beyond the human manifestation of God, to also understand Jesus as a representative of the cosmic *Logos*. The Greek concept of *Logos* — λόγος — weakly translated into English as "The Word," is the reasoning principle and creative part of God. The Apostle

John employed the word to connect the Incarnate Jesus with the Creator Yahweh. "In the beginning was the Word (Logos), and the Word (Logos) was with God, and the Word (Logos) was God. He [Christ Jesus] was in the beginning with God. All things came into being through him ... In him was life, and that life was the light of all ..."[149] That is a quantum leap from the primitive, folklore myths of a god-man, such as Zeus or Thor.

Incarnate and Invisible: Paradox within Paradox

God chooses to remain mysterious and invisible ... *and* chooses to be revealed via Creation and Incarnation. A paradox if ever there was one. Jesus said, "I and the Father [the Godhead] are one." For centuries, theologians tried to imagine how all of God could be poured into a single human figure walking the earth for just 33 years. One of my favorite seminary professors, the late Dr. William Mallard, gave this example ... it sounded like a joke, but it had no punchline:

"A man walks into an ice cream store and asks for a gallon of vanilla and a gallon of chocolate. The vendor hands him two gallon-containers, one white, one brown. 'No,' the customer says, 'I want them in a single container.' So, the vendor reaches for a single gallon of marbled ice cream: chocolate and vanilla swirled together. 'No,' the customer again demurs. 'I want a full gallon of vanilla and a full gallon of chocolate, but I want them in one, single, gallon container.' The ice cream vendor throws his hands up in despair, and runs the customer off." Dr. Mallard concluded, "This is the doctrine of the Incarnation: all of God poured into a single human container. Jesus. Fully human and fully divine."[150] Martin Luther put it this way: "The mystery of the humanity of Christ, that He sunk Himself into our flesh, is beyond human understanding."[151]

As with all concepts, there are paradoxes within paradoxes. I'm not alone in believing that God made an explicit effort to become known to us via the Incarnate Christ. But I must concede that the revelation of Jesus is limited, primarily because Jesus no longer stands before us in a physical form (other than in "ink": the story of his life and person in the gospels). So, there is the additional paradox: God has Self-revealed, yet God has Self-obscured. Before I attempt to answer "Why?", allow me another digression.

A Grand Purpose Revealed in Cosmic Order?

The amazing order of the universe seems to indicate a Grand Purpose behind it all. Philosophers debate this, but it seems intrinsically true. Chaos strikes me as the opposite of purpose. Flat stones lined up in a row leading to a doorway are likely purposefully placed stepping stones; similar stones scattered randomly in a dried creek-bed do not seem to have significant purpose (Taoism aside). Terrestrial Life, and especially human consciousness, would not exist without the exact formulation of certain complex orderings: the proper size and location of a fusion generator (our Sun); the orbit and rotation of our planet (meeting the temperature requirements of mammals); the ratios of gasses in our atmosphere (particularly nitrogen to oxygen); the size/mass of our planet (proper gravity to retain atmosphere); the factors that protect us from space radiation and excessive bombardment via asteroids (thank you, Jupiter!); photosynthesis; water (its quantity and characteristics). The list goes on.

I have only scratched the surface with this list of the incredible coincidences (or purposeful fine-tuning?) necessary for advanced life to exist. Cambridge University astrophysicist Fred Hoyle cited another such singularity in his own work: only one very specific resonance of energy and spin within a carbon atom's nucleus can allow for the formation of carbon from helium in solar fusion. Hoyle stated that without the nucleus spinning at that specific frequency, the quantities of carbon in the universe would have been too small for carbon-based life forms to exist (remember, the carbon in your body was once a star!). This fact is so statistically unlikely, Hoyle suggested that "some super-calculating intellect must have designed the properties of the carbon atom, otherwise the chance of my finding such an atom through the blind forces of nature would be utterly minuscule."[152]

Minuscule is an understatement. Hoyle was also a mathematician, so he was able to calculate that for life on earth to exist by random chance evolution, the odds are one in $10^{40,000}$ (that is, without either a "designer" or some kind of extraterrestrial "panspermia" from ancient aliens).[153] Cut his estimate in half, and that's still a number so big, it can't be used to actually *count* anything, as it greatly exceeds the number of all the atoms in the cosmos (approx. 10^{80}). Professor Hoyle pointed to this sublime order of the universe and said, "A common sense interpretation of the facts suggests that a super-intellect has monkeyed with physics, as well as with chemistry and biology, and that there are no blind forces worth speaking about in nature. The numbers … seem to me so overwhelming as to put this conclusion almost beyond question."[154] This is not the biased argument of a "Creationist"; the late Professor Hoyle was an agnostic.

The Purposeful Creator's *Purpose* in Hiding

So it seems that a central trait of our Creator God is *Purposeful Design*. From there I will make the next assumption: a purposeful God has sound reasons for playing "Hide and Seek" with us. Because God does not "prove Himself" to skeptics, they doubt God's existence. But God has motives for not revealing every secret of Eternity.

Historically, theologians and philosophers have proposed several answers as to why God may purposefully, partially, hide from us.

1. Our Finitude: Obviously, our brains are finite. That which is finite cannot possibly grasp or contain all of the Infinite.

2. The Game: God wants us to enjoy the process of growing and expanding our knowledge, slowly. Yes, God may actually want us to have *fun* in this existence! A quick example: at times when my work schedule interfered with watching my alma mater play college football, I've had to record the game and watch it later. But then if I accidentally overheard the final score before viewing the game, it spoiled the experience. It's simply not as much fun to participate in a game (as a spectator or a player) if the outcome is known in advance.

3. Free Will: It seems that God's design and purpose includes making us something more than robots or puppets. God wishes for us to be free moral agents, free to stand apart from the Creator. If God were to fully self-reveal — with all the power of the universe standing before us — we might freeze in total fear and overwhelming awe.

4. Mystery: Why there remains so much Mystery about God could itself be a mystery that we are not yet entitled to know.

All of this is to say that there is nothing irrational about believing in a Creator Being. Our lack of understanding or proof of the Supernatural does not constitute a reason to doubt. It is not necessary to have all the answers in order to have belief/ faith. Moreover, there is nothing intellectually superior about the position of atheists. They don't know a thing more than we (i.e. people of faith) do. Acknowledging paradoxes — aspects of God that seem enigmatic and even contradictory — actually points to a higher reasoning process, not to a primitive ignorance. There is a world of difference between *Superstition* and *Supernatural*.

A Natural God ... and the Quantum View

We may eventually learn that the things appearing to be unknowable or supernatural are all still part of a "natural" universe. That would not rule out the existence and activity of God ... God is, in the highest sense, as natural as any other phenomenon in a galaxy filled with paradox. Quantum Theory can help us understand how these paradoxes may be possible.

(If you've not yet read the Preface to this book, now is a good time to do so ... but I will expand some of those ideas here in this final chapter.) Science and religion hopefully will arrive at the same destination, the same conclusion. For now, I call this the "Quantum View," as I keep bumping into concepts in quantum theories that reflect concepts found in Scripture.

Jesus reminded us that a tiny seed contains all the information necessary to create a tree. In a similar way, physicist David Bohm observed that tiny quanta contain, or reflect, structural information almost infinitely bigger than the sub-atomic particles. Bohm may have exaggerated when he said, "Everything is enfolded into everything." But he used holograms as a metaphor of how this might work. In a true 3-D holographic image, any one part of the hologram contains all the data of the whole hologram. Physicist Bohm asserted that reality, in a sense, is a holographic image, and the whole image can be projected in a single quantum packet — a single ray of light. Centuries ago, the Christian mystic, Gregory the Great, tried to describe a religious vision this way: it was as if "the whole world [was] gathered ... under one ray of the sun." Quantum physicists say it less poetically.

Even without knowing about holograms, Leonardo Da Vinci showed how a primitive *camera obscura* could turn a single ray of light into a tableau — for example, a landscape view shining through a pinhole projects the entire countryside onto a darkened wall. Bohm also said that light is "the fundamental activity in which existence has its ground." Jesus said, "I am the light of the world." And if you prefer poets over scientists, consider Walt Whitman's words: "I believe a leaf of grass is no less than the journey-work of the stars ... or a grain of sand ... All truths wait in all things."[155]Or Ephesians 1:23: "... the fullness of [Christ] is filling the all in all." Or William Blake's vision: "To see a world in a grain of sand, and heaven in a wildflower ... to hold infinity in the palm of your hand."[156] Neither Whitman nor Blake had any notion of the miracle of DNA, a microscopic speck that holds all the information necessary to create an entire human being.

Even Poets Could Not Imagine Today's Quantum View

Bohm tied that holistic principle of "undivided wholeness" with the idea that everything is in *a process of becoming*, a "dynamic wholeness-in-motion" in which everything moves together in an interconnected process. He stated that "elementary particles are actually systems of extremely complicated internal structure, acting essentially as amplifiers of information contained in a quantum wave," adding that this ultra-holistic cosmic view means that everything is connected with everything else. To repeat, Bohm theorized that any individual element could reveal "detailed information about every other element in the universe" and the "unbroken wholeness of the totality of existence" could be seen as "an undivided flowing movement without borders." Underlying it is a deeper order of existence, a primary level of reality that gives shape to the things we see in our physical world. Bohm called the unseen, deeper level of reality — the enfolded data — the *Implicate Order*, and our observation of the "holographic projection" or visual level of reality that unfolds before us, he named the *Explicate Order*. As the late Michael Talbot put it, "protons, electrons, photons, *et cetera* are no more substantive or permanent than the form a geyser of water takes as it gushes out of a fountain. The water droplets fall back into the pool and disappear, but do not die. When a particle appears to be destroyed, it is not lost. It has merely enfolded back into the deeper order from which it sprang."[157]

The Miracle of Life

The cutting edge of science is slicing through old boundaries. The dissection reveals that everything is bigger, more complex, and yes, more "mystical" or "metaphysical" (for lack of better words) than natural science had imagined prior to the twentieth century. One of the more interesting aspects of quantum research is that it is not just looking at outer space, but is peering intensely into inner space. The miracle of life has not been reduced to a simple genetic code; we are discovering more layers of molecular biology, and deeper atomic action. The researchers are finding subatomic, quantum information behind the workings of life, from the cellular level all the way up to the operations of the human brain.

Matthew Fisher, a physicist at the University of California, is one of several scientists working in the emerging field of "quantum neuroscience." Quantum neuroscience understands that the brain is far more intricate than a digital computer; the brain is not just a fancy MacBook running on binary code, it is a *quantum* computer. In recent years, evidence suggests that all advanced biological systems employ quantum mechanics: **photosynthesis** (see the work of Alexandra Olaya-Castro, a physicist at University College, London); **birds' navigation/ migratory sensors** (*magnetodetection* — see the work of University of Oxford chemist Peter Hore), **olfactory abilities** (see the Endnotes re: a paper by Harini and Sowdhamini), and more.[158]

Professor Birgitta Whaley, University of California, Berkeley, believes that quantum physicist Erwin Schrödinger was right in his pioneering work on quantum biology. The labyrinthine structures of living organisms go way beyond what scientists first believed. DNA does not function via a mere handful (so to speak) of molecular bonds, but utilizes complex quantum processes. She cites the fact that photosynthesizing bacteria use quantum decoherence to "speed up the transfer of electronic information by accessing vibrational energies" to enhance the process of photosynthesis "with a very high rate of efficiency [using] quantum mechanical tricks that we cannot yet replicate in machines."[159]

Entanglement, Not Dichotomy

The size and the interconnectedness of the universe go beyond anything classical orthodoxy (in art, science or religion) could have dreamed just 200 years ago. As psychologist Carl Jung predicted, when he wrote about "Collective Consciousness," that the elements of the universe are intertwined across time and space in a way that previously could only be described as God-like. Incidentally, I think of Dr. Jung as the first "quantum psychologist." Even when discussing dichotomies, Jung avoids the oversimplification of dualism; he described paired matters as *syzygies*, implying the original Greek meaning of the word as something relational, something "yoked together." This in turn evokes the idea of quantum entanglement of two particles. To reiterate from a previous chapter: Quantum Entanglement was at first as "unbelievable" as skeptics and materialists claim prayer and supernatural miracles to be. When particles are entangled, it means that information is transferred between them instantaneously, even thousands of miles apart. This has been proven in more than one actual experiment. Dr. Bohm went further, saying that entangled sub-atomic particles "respond to each other's motions thousands of years later [even] when they are light-years apart."

Hocus Pocus or Sober Science?

Yes, it all sounds quite mystical. That does not mean "New Age," a "spiritual" movement that is too often associated with unscientific nonsense and questionable self-styled "gurus" and kooky cults. When I speak of Christian mysticism, it is rooted in the unselfish, sober and sensible monastic mystics, like Thomas Merton, Gregory of Nyssa, Teresa Avila, Evagrius Ponticus, *et al.* Nor am I speaking of mystical in the sense of a Pentecostal emotional experience (though certainly you will come a lot closer to having a mystical, ecstatic encounter with God if you open up your heart and emotions). The *American Heritage*

Dictionary defines mystical as: "having a spiritual reality ... not apparent to the intelligence or senses ... stemming from direct communion with God ..." Poet Samuel Taylor Coleridge said that for someone to have poetic-metaphysical vision, one must exert a "willing suspension of disbelief." We have to be willing to think outside the box, to contemplate the infinite, to open ourselves up to all possibilities. Most people don't see it; most never witness the mystery. They are stuck in the ordinary. They scoff at the miraculous.

Miracles on Main Street

Miracles abound. And children know it. For example, you can see it in their twinkling eyes at Christmastime. They intuitively know it's more than just toys and tinsel. They know there is something magical about Christmas, even before they truly understand that the Nativity story is about a quantum event of God pouring God's self into a tiny baby in a manger. Christmas is also a paradox, by the way.

Allow me to retell my favorite illustration of childlike wonder, from a fun movie, "Blast from the Past." Adam Webber had lived in an underground blast shelter for all of his 30 years. His parents had mistaken a jet plane crash for a nuclear apocalypse, and kept Adam underground in their elaborate bomb shelter. For decades, they kept him isolated from the real world until the "radiation" levels became safe. So finally, still childlike and naive, 30-year-old Adam steps out and views sunshine and blue sky for the first time in his life. He is astounded at the indescribable, infinite blue beauty arching above him and exclaims in wonder, "My gosh, look at that! It's *amazing!*"

A woman passerby sees him pointing to an empty sky and says glumly, "What? I don't see anything." And he exclaims and gestures again, "The sky!" She says, "I still don't get it." But the lady's 5-year-old daughter looks up, points at the halcyon blue panorama ... and with a twinkle in her eye, announces with glee,

"I see it! I see it!" Enough said.

Centuries ago, Matthew Henry wrote this commentary regarding Christ's words in the Gospel of Matthew, Chapter 18: "Our Lord set a little child before them, solemnly assuring them, that unless they [changed and became] like little children, they could not enter his kingdom. Children, when very young, do not desire authority, do not regard outward distinctions, are free from malice, are teachable and willingly dependent on their parents ... [thus are] proper emblems of the [humble] minds of true Christians. Surely we need to be daily renewed in the spirit of our minds, that we may become simple and humble, as little children, and willing to be the least of all."[160]

As author Nikos Kazantzakis put it, "nothing more resembles God's eyes than the eyes of a child," because each and every time they look around, "they see the world for the first time."

Questions for Thought, Study and Group Discussion

How do you define a "miracle"? Have you ever personally witnessed, or had first-hand experience with, something you might deem a miracle?

When you close your eyes and hear the word "God," do you have a mental picture? If so, is that mental picture of God different from, or similar to, an image formed in your mind as a child? Discuss.

Early in this chapter, the author suggests four reasons or explanations as to why God may purposefully hide from us. Discuss which of those four (*Our Finitude, the Game, Free Will, Mystery*) seem most satisfactory or probable to you.

Paradox 11

The Created can come to know the Creator; the Finite can glimpse the Infinite; yet Mystery remains.

Reflective Quote for Chapter 11

My own suspicion is that the universe is not only queerer than we suppose, but queerer than we **can** suppose."

~ *J. B. S. Haldane, Scottish mathematical biologist, in a time when "queer"meant "strange and odd."*

Conclusion

Contraria Sunt Complementa
~ family motto of Niels Bohr, physicist

Appreciating and understanding Paradox does not mean blindly accepting contradictory nonsense. With musical chords (three or more keys played simultaneously), harmony and dissonance are but a single note apart. We could play two notes in the context of a particular scale, and depending on the scale, those same two notes can be either *dissonant* — clashing horribly with each other — or *harmonious* and pleasing. Music is amazing in that way. **The beauty is inseparable from the context.** The same is true when speaking of paradox: we cannot just grab two illogical axioms, stick them together without context and call that "a grand paradoxical truth." Employing paradox as a revelatory tool requires intelligent consideration of context and intent.

Premature satiation or "settling" on one side of a duality is unhealthy. The goal is to embrace the tension of it, as with a Jungian syzygy, holding onto it as an intact paradox. The aim is not to "settle" on one side or the other, but to transcend the syzygy and understand (but not separate) the entangled twins *in toto*. Then we can discern something much bigger and holistic — something closer to Truth. The only acceptable resolution to a spiritual Paradox is Transcendence.

Spiritually/theologically-speaking, the obvious example or metaphor is *Law vs. Grace* ... the classic Paradox in Christian theology. If a person "settles" only on the side of Law, he/she becomes a judgmental Fundamentalist; if one settles only on Grace, one can fall into a meaningless, vague New Age pop-philosophy that says, "I'm okay, you're okay." (Cannibal Jeffrey Dahmer, for example, was certainly *not* okay.)

The more common "sin" when it comes to biblical paradoxes

and contradictions is to quickly accept one side of the paradox, bolster it with sympathetic verses that fit a person's bias, and then vehemently reject the other side — attacking dissenters as wrong, demonic, or worse yet (in the eyes of the Rightwing Christian) ... Liberal!

My hope is that my personal blemishes, biases and beliefs will not cause readers to dismiss whatever truths can be gleaned from this book. Labeling me as an Apostate, Liberal, Pantheist, Heretic, or New Ager would be inaccurate and unhelpful. To be accurate, I am a Bible-believing Christian. Jesus has always been and shall always be the manifestation of God that best "works" for me. At the same time, I cannot accept that a loving God will condemn to a fiery Hades those who sincerely approach the Divine from other traditions. Humility with Faith is yet another paradox, a balancing act between wanting to share what I've experienced of a Loving and Forgiving God (embodied and revealed in the historical person of Jesus of Nazareth), without trying to impose my views arrogantly upon others.

Having been raised in the Church, the son of a Methodist minister, and a pastor myself, it may seem that I acquired faith easily or automatically. *Au contraire!* I've gone through many a "dark night of the soul," periods of agnosticism, with doubts and troubled times when I would be tearfully angry at God for allowing all the suffering on this planet.

As her pastor, I watched with dismay as a young nurse in our church became paralyzed in a car accident. She was pregnant at the time, but because of the trauma, miscarried. Her quadriplegia was of the most severe kind, dependent on a constant life support machine, and she was not able to communicate vocally. The unrelenting prayers and pleadings of the congregation — including "saints" far more dedicated than I — went seemingly unanswered. She died after a few years of suffering. It was one of a long list of tragedies during my pastoral "watch" of 28 years ... inexplicable tragedies that happened to "good people."

Reading Rabbi Harold Kusner's excellent book, *When Bad Things Happen to Good People*, and other books like it, did not assuage my feelings that God had let us down.

Nevertheless, I still believe in the miraculous, and in a loving God. I believe in eternal life and eternal love. The answer to many prayers comes after we cross the threshold to the next dimension.

Playwright Thornton Wilder wrote, "There is a land of the living and a land of the dead and the bridge is love, the only survival, the only meaning." Without love, we will wither and die — figuratively if you don't believe in an afterlife; literally if you do. Without love, no life is possible beyond this one. The predominant themes in the teachings of Jesus are variations of "Love your neighbor as yourself."[161] The Apostle Paul echoed this in Galatians: "The only thing that counts is faith expressing itself through love.[162] For the entire law is fulfilled in keeping this one command: "Love your neighbor as yourself."[163]

Peel away everything else in the Christian religion and we find the core of it is Love. By comparison, all the other accoutrements and doctrinal minutiae are as ugly as a barnacled oyster shell … within which is the sparkling, perfect Pearl of Great Price. Is it heresy to suggest that we focus on the Pearl? The shell — by which I mean the barnacles of orthodoxy and an old, calcified institution called the Church — helped form and deliver the Pearl to us, and yes, it brought us the meat of the oyster (i.e. canonized Scripture). But only a fool would discard the Pearl and keep the shell.

The Pearl of Great Price is the love of God embodied in Jesus and in the Two Great Commandments. Jesus repeatedly encouraged us to seek the Pearl above all else. Consider Jesus' words, "Seek first His kingdom and His righteousness."[164] Remember that Jesus described himself as the embodiment of the "Kingdom of Heaven" (the essence of God), and receive this truth: "Again, the kingdom of heaven is like a merchant seeking beautiful pearls, who, when he had found one Pearl of Great Price, went and sold all that he had and bought it."[165]

Bobby

On the topic of God's love, one of my earliest and best experiences in ministry came in teaching a young boy, Bobby, in Vacation Bible School and later in Confirmation Class. Bobby, I was told, was "retarded," the word commonly used back then. He had the intellectual ability of a First Grader, barely able to read and write the simplest of words. But he participated fully in class, and when the class ended, I told all my 12-year-old students: "Next Sunday, you will be invited to stand before the church and profess your Christian faith, making the vows of membership to become full 'adult' members of the Church. This is not your parents' decision. It is yours and yours alone. I'd like to think it is your first step toward becoming an adult ... so you can say, 'Yes, I'd like to do that,' or 'No, I'm not ready,' or whatever you wish." Bobby said yes.

So the next Sunday, I presented the Confirmation Class before the congregation. I asked them the questions of membership, wording them in ways that Bobby could understand. He proudly proclaimed, "Yes" and the other appropriate answers to church membership vows. I had also asked each Confirmation Class-member to choose a short Bible verse, hopefully one of their favorites, and recite it aloud from memory during the ritual. I asked Bobby to memorize a three-word Scripture from The Fourth Letter of John: "God is love." Bobby recited the words before his family and friends and fellow parishioners with a huge smile, a twinkle in his eyes, and a life that embodied that very thing called Love. Everyone there loved Bobby, because he was both very lovable and very love-giving. Intellectually, he could not have grasped the paradoxes explicated in this book. But he understood Love.

I sometimes whimsically wondered if the author Winston

Groom had somehow stolen the idea for his character, Forrest Gump, from my experiences with Bobby. Because I had frequently said: "Bobby may not understand all the details of church doctrine, but he sure does understand the core truth, that *God is Love!*" A key scene in the movie *Forrest Gump* brings me to tears because it reminds me of the sweet soul of Bobby. Forrest Gump was answering his lifelong love, Jenny, who had accused him of not having the intellectual capacity to truly be "in love." He said, with an impassioned, affected Southern voice not much different from Bobby's: "I'm not a smart man, but I know what Love is!"

I am no genius, and certainly no saint, but I know what Love is. And like Bobby, I know that God is Love.

Previous Books by this Author

End of the World Propheteers
Exposing the Truth about Apocalyptic Predictions and the Blood Moon Scam

Killing JFK: 50 Years, 50 Lies
From the Warren Commission to Bill O'Reilly, A History of Deceit in the Kennedy Assassination

Class Crucifixion
Money, Power, Religion and the Death of the Middle Class

Majestic Twelve Minus One
(Fiction)

The Neurotic's Guide to God and Love
Seven Mistakes that Make Us Crazy, and Eight Ways to Change

Outdoors with God
Devotional Thoughts on the Great Outdoors

Firm Foundations
An Architect and a Pastor Guide Your Church Construction
(co-authored with Dan Michal)

Endnotes

1   See the works of quantum physicists Erwin Schrödinger and/or Werner Heisenberg, re: how observation changes reality ("The Observer Effect").

2   Devout Mormons (now officially known as members of The Church of Jesus Christ of Latter-day Saints) wear a unique type of underwear called a "temple garment." Presidential candidate Mitt Romney discussed the rationale for his sacred underwear on the campaign trail in 2016.

3   www.bbc.com/news/world-33256561
    BBC article documents the steep and steady decline of "practicing Christians" in Europe (percentage-wise over decades). While several factors are involved, surveys and studies have identified post-modern sensibilities and the rise in scientific knowledge chief causes.

4   www.pewforum.org/2015/05/12/americas-changing-religious-landscape/

5   Matthew 11:30 (See verses 11:28–30)

See Notes about Bible Copyrights, Quotations and Sources at end of Endnotes.

6   See Luke 11:46 for one of several such criticisms of the Sadducees and Pharisees.

7   Matthew 11:30, but the original Greek behind the phrase "my yoke is easy" is literally "fits well."

8   Matthew 11:29

9   Jennifer Oulette, "Spooky Quantum Action Might Hold the Universe Together,"*Quanta Magazine* (May 2015). Accessed here: www.wired.com/2015/05/spooky-quantum-action-might-hold-universe-together

10 Matthew 17:20

11 www.wired.com/2015/05/spooky-quantum-action-might-

hold-universe-together

12   Ephesians 1:9–11, excerpted, and Colossians 3:12b

13   Conservative Scholar Kenneth Mathews makes a strong argument that the first half of Genesis is, paradoxically, both history and myth/parable. See Kenneth Mathews *Genesis 1–11: An Exegetical and Theological Exposition of Holy Scripture*, in *The New American Commentary* series, (Holman Reference, 1996). I find that to be more intellectually honest than the false dichotomy (and one-sided assertions) by "Young Earth Creationist" Del Tackett of "Focus on the Family's" *Truth Project*. Here's a link to an informed Christian's response to Tackett:

www.biologos.org/blogs/guest/a-former-young-earth-creationist-responds-to-is-genesis-history

14   From the Greek word "to know." The religious Gnostics were a part of the so-called "Secret Mystery Religions" of ancient Egypt and Greece, who sought enlightenment via a "secret knowledge", imparted through a lengthy Initiation ritual ... sometimes even involving hallucinogenic drugs. One medieval painting portrayed Adam and Eve beside the Tree of the Knowledge of Good and Evil ... but instead of red apples, the fruit is the red "sacred mushroom" *Amanita muscaria*, which induces hallucinogenic visions.

15   Isaiah 1:18, KJV

16   Proverbs 13:20

17   Job 38:31

18   *Theodicy* attempts to explain the paradox of how/why an all-loving, all-powerful God allows evil and suffering.

19   Quantum physicists Bohm, Heisenberg, Schrödinger, Niels Bohr, *et al.*, have all identified key paradoxes in physics, and/or use the word *paradox* to describe significant aspects of quantum mechanics.

20   For a beginner's read on cosmic paradoxes, see the essay, "What Are the Paradoxes in Quantum Mechanics?" by

Allan Steinhardt, PhD, a chief scientist at DARPA, found here:
www.forbes.com/sites/quora/2016/11/03/what-are-the-paradoxes-in-quantum-mechanics/#5d17c2f612d6

21 Matthew 18:3

22 Matthew 18:4

23 Isaiah 1:18 KJV

24 Re: Jacob wrestling God, an angel, or a demon, see
www.rabbimichaelsamuel.com/2009/03/who-did-jacob-really-wrestle-with-in-the-bible/

25 Romans 6:22

26 After writing most of this book, I stumbled upon the writings of theologian Richard Rohr. His work assures me I'm not alone in my understanding. Here is the larger context of what I quoted from him, in his book, *Holding the Tension: The Power of Paradox*: "God is the only one we can surrender to without losing ourselves. In fact, we find our deepest, truest, and most loving self in God. Yet it is still a paradox. [All] true spirituality has the character of paradox to it, precisely because it is always holding together the Whole of Reality ... Everything in this world is both attractive and non-attractive, light and darkness, passing and eternal, life and death — at the same time ... Everything has different sides, levels, truths, perspectives ... A paradox is something that appears to be a contradiction, but from another perspective is not a contradiction at all. You and I are living paradoxes ... If you can hold and forgive the contradictions within yourself, you can normally do it everywhere else, too. If you cannot do it within yourself, you will actually ... project dichotomies everywhere else."

Rohr has also written similar thoughts on the subject of ego surrender. He states: "God is the only one we can surrender to without losing ourselves. In fact, we find our deepest, truest, and most loving self in God. Yet it is still a paradox." Rohr's words are a good reflection of my opening quote from Carl Jung on Paradox (in my Preface), so not surprisingly, Rohr also touches on other themes of my book: the challenge of surrendering Ego without losing Self; the limits of dualism/dichotomies; the need to surrender ego-centric biases.

27 www.cbsnews.com/news/vatican-reveals-how-many-priests-defrocked-for-sex-abuse-since-2004/

28 Luke 11:46

29 Romans 12:2, J.B. Phillips paraphrase

30 John Wesley, "A Plain Account of Christian Perfection," (tract published in London, 1777).

31 1st John 4:11 and 5:2

32 www.abcnews.go.com/US/snake-handling-pentecostal-pastor-dies-snake-bite/story?id=22551754

33 The term "jihad" can mean a holy battle against infidels, or it can allegorically mean a holy struggle for right spirituality. For one answer as to how non-Fundamentalist Islamists understand these contextually, see: www.aboutjihad.com/terrorism/quran_misquote_part_2.php

34 www.apologeticspress.org/apcontent.aspx?category=6&article=542

35 Carbon-14 dating is often an approximation, and has, at times, generated conflicting dates. See R. E. Taylor, *Radiocarbon Dating*, (Academic Press, London, 1987, pp. 125–126. Even staunch defenders of science admit that other tools must be used to date rocks older than 70,000 years old: www.actionbioscience.org/evolution/benton.html

36 Genesis 6:20

37 Genesis 7:21

38 It rained for 40 days, but the animals were inside the Ark for over a year, according to Genesis. www.arkonararat.com/Timeline.html and Genesis 8.

39 www.creationproof.com/id30.html

40 Charlotte Lindqvista, *et al.*, "Complete mitochondrial genome of a Pleistocene jawbone unveils the origin of polar bear," paper published by the National Academy of Sciences, March 16, 2010.

41 Joshua 10:13

42 Joshua 10:11

43 2nd Timothy 3:16, NRSV

44 Matthew 5:17–18

45 Mark 10:18: "… only God is good." Greek *agathos*, meaning good or excellent or perfect.

46 www.collective-evolution.com/2014/09/27/this-is-the-world-of-quantum-physics-nothing-is-solid-and-everything-is-energy

47 www.scribd.com/document/146495774/small-creation-myths-of-the-world

48 Proverbs 1:7a

49 Acts 9:31; 2nd Corinthians 5:11, examined below.

50 *The Interpreter's Dictionary of the Bible*, (Abingdon Press, 1962), pp. 257–259.

51 Psalm 2:11, NLT

52 Luke 1:2–19

53 Luke 2:8–10

54 2nd Corinthians 5:11

55 2nd Corinthians 5:17,19b

56 Alfred North Whitehead, *Science and the Modern World* (The Free Press, New York, 1967), p. 17, and *Process and Reality*, (Free Press, 1978), pp. 208.

57 Clement of Alexandria, *The Stromata*, Book 6, Chapter 16, (205 CE).

58 See www.joeledmundanderson.com/?p=666

59 See *Spirit and Letter in Origen and Augustine*, Paul Fiddes, Editor (T&T Clark, 2013). See pp. 87–90, contributions by Morwenna Ludlow.

60 Origen, *De Principiis* (Book IV), p. 16.

61 Galatians 4:24, KJV

62 Using Old Testament non-inclusive language here.

63 Matthew 15:21–28

64 Ecclesiastes 3:11, NRSV

65 *The Androgyny of Jesus*, by V. R. Mollenkott, in Volume 2, Number 2 of *Daughters of Sarah* magazine, March, 1976.

66 Herbert W. Armstrong's "Worldwide Church of God" is one of the rare exceptions, as he tried to re-institute Judaism (a "Christianized" Judaism) amongst his followers.

67 The changeability vs. static nature of God is less of an issue for most Eastern religions.

68 www.livescience.com/32660-how-does-an-atomic-clock-work.html

69 www.exactlywhatistime.com/physics-of-time/relativistic-time/

70 ww.religion.blogs.cnn.com/2011/05/12/religious-belief-is-human-nature-huge-new-study-claims/

71 Psychosocial stages, as described by both, can be found in James Fowler's book, *Stages of Faith*, (HarperCollins, San Francisco, 1995).

72 Luke 24:46–47

73 Matthew 18:21-22; Luke 17:3–4

74 Matthew 6:14–15

75 Luke 6:37

76 Matthew 18:35

77 Luke 23:34

78 This is my paraphrase of Luke 6:31.

79 Revelation 3:20, NKJV

80 Genesis 1:27, 31, NRSV

81 From the book, *On the Incarnation*, ca. 318 CE, by Athanasius of Alexandria ... which C. S. Lewis called "a masterpiece."

82 Christopher Lasch, *The Culture of Narcissism*, (Norton & Co., New York, 1991).

83 Matthew 22:37–39

84   John 15:13

85   Martin Luther King, Jr., *Strength to Love*, (Fortress Press, 2010), p. 26.

86   James Herriot, *All Creatures Great and Small*, (St. Martin's Press, London, 2014 ed.).

87   Carl G. Jung, *The Collected Works of C. G. Jung* (Vol. 6), (Bollingen, 1976), para 797.

88   Eckhart Tolle, *A New Earth*, (Penguin Books, NY, 2015), excerpts from pp. 27–28, my annotations in [brackets].

89   Johann Hari, *Lost Connections*, (Bloomsbury USA Publishing, NY, 2018), Chapter 8.

90   Ibid

91   Ibid

92   Ibid, p. 182. Emphasis mine.

93   Like Rohr, I love that poetic phrase used by Gerard Manly Hopkins, *immortal diamond*, from Hopkins' poem, *That Nature Is a Heraclitean Fire and of the Comfort of the Resurrection*.

94   1st Timothy 4:8

95   1st Corinthians 6:19

96   David Loy, *Lack and Transcendence: The Problem of Death and Life in Psychotherapy, Existentialism, and Buddhism*, (Humanity Books, 2000).

97   David Loy article here: www.zen-occidental.net/articles1/loy14-eng.html

98   Jin Y. Park, *Buddhisms* [sic] *and Deconstructions*, (Rowman & Littlefield, 2006), p. 79.

99   Dionysius the Areopagite, in his book, *Mystical Theology*.

100 *The Interior Castle*, St. Teresa of Ávila, 1577, Chapter 2.

101 John 3:7

102 John 12:24

103 Philippians 2:5–9, NIV, annotated/excerpted.

104 Ephesians 4:22–24, NAS excerpted.

105 John 13:14–15

106 Revelation 2:17, from the original Greek.

107 *The Mounce Reverse-Interlinear New Testament*, ed. Robert H. Mounce and William D. Mounce, 2011.

108 www.fralfonse.blogspot.com/2011/01/mk-51-20-man-in-chains.html

109 www.christianhistoryinstitute.org/magazine/article/three-views-of-hell

110 *International Standard Bible Encyclopedia*, ed. James Orr (Chicago: Howard-Severance Co., 1915)

111 www.newyorker.com/magazine/2012/11/26/the-hell-raiser-3

112 On "Palm Sunday," Jesus made a so-called Triumphal Entry into downtown Jerusalem riding on a donkey colt, making a satire of triumphant processions by rulers on mighty steeds … almost as comical as a clown coming into the circus ring squeezed into a tiny clown car.

113 Colossians 1:19–20, NIV and CEV

114 Romans 14:11

115 Titus 2:11 (CEV), emphasis mine.

116 John 12:32

117 2nd Thessalonians 1:8–9, excerpted

118 I am not endorsing these sites, but their lay-accessible explanations regarding the meaning of *aion/aionio* and eternal punishment are helpful: www.godsplanforall.com/free-online-book/part-ii/chapter-17-translations-of-owlam-aion-and-aionios/
And/or: www.patheos.com/blogs/unfundamentalistchristians/2017/04/indeed-many-universalism-early-church/#2JLZtD6e1W7jxWLq.99

119 William Barclay, *New Testament Words*, (Westminster John Knox Press, 1976), p. 37.

120 From *Strong's Exhaustive Concordance*, re: Greek word G931.

121 Malachi 3:1–3

122 1st Timothy 2:4, NRSV

123 Matthew 16:18, excerpted

124 A few examples of where science may be hinting at signs of immortality or life beyond our immediate physical existence: Consider cutting-edge DNA research. DNA contains vast quantum information, far more than simple chromosome traits, and DNA is now considered the best long-term storage medium for information, with storage longevity of a million years, according to Dr. Robert N. Grass of ETH Zurich. For other examples, consider the theories about a multiverse (an existence that transcends this reality, which is not a long way from how we might define Heaven), or the topic "temporal extension of particles."

125 See: Jerry Fodor and Massimo Piattelli-Palmarini, *What Darwin Got Wrong*, (Picador, 2011). The authors report that cutting-edge biology is moving away from simple natural selection, towards a mixed endogenous/exogenous model of how biological change occurs. To say that Darwinism is outdated is **not** to say that Evolution doesn't happen, nor is it a religious argument; the authors (F & P-P) are atheists. For a more philosophical take, try *Mind & Cosmos: Why the Materialist Neo-Darwinian Conception of Nature is Almost Certainly False*, by Thomas Nagel. Nagel is also an atheist, but his work is less polemical than that of Richard Dawkins (Materialist) or William Dembski (Creationist). Nagel rises above the religious debate surrounding Darwinism, and it is striking that as an atheist, he states in his Conclusion that Darwinian orthodoxy "will seem laughable in a generation or two." Another "middle-ground" book on this unnecessarily controversial topic is: *Evolution 2.0*, by Perry Marshall.

126 Galileo's Letter to Johannes Kepler (1610), found in *The Crime of Galileo*, by Giorgio De Santillana, 1955.

127 www.samharris.org/science-must-destroy-religion/

128 Gary B. Ferngren, *Science & Religion: A Historical Introduction*.

(Johns Hopkins University Press, Baltimore, 2002), see pp. 20–23.

129 See Augustine and Anselm.

130 www.health.harvard.edu/heart-health/are-eggs-risky-for-heart-health

131 Henry Margenau in his article "Why I Am a Christian," in the magazine *Truth*, Vol. 1, 1985.

132 Immanuel Kant, *Critique of Pure Reason*, (Cambridge University Press,1999); quote is from the Preface to the Second Edition.

133 www.sciencemag.org/news/2017/06/china-s-quantum-satellite-achieves-spooky-action-record-distance

134 www.wired.com/2011/01/timelike-entanglement

135 The classic "voodoo doll" supposedly functions like an Entanglement: the witch doctor makes an effigy or "twin" of someone, and then when a pin is stuck in the doll's arm, the human feels the same action at a distance. I don't believe in voodoo, and I find Quantum Entanglement to be nearly as fantastical!

136 Jennifer Oulette, "How Quantum Pairs Stitch Space," *Quanta Magazine* (April 2015). Accessed here: www.linkis.com/quantamagazine.org/3nnyJ

137 John 1:1, excerpted. See more on "Logos" in the final chapter of this book.

138 Evelyn Underhill, *Mysticism: A Study in the Nature and Development of Spiritual Consciousness*, (Dover Publications, 2002), p. 4.

139 2 Corinthians 3:3

140 Romans 2:29

141 Catholics and Protestants agree that the Apocrypha has lesser authority than the 66 canonical books.

142 Augustine of Hippo, *Commentary on the Book of Genesis*, Chapter 18, (415 CE).

143 Acts 2:3–4

144 www.scientificamerican.com/article/how-fast-is-the-earth-mov/

145 See Luke 5:36–37

146 Leonard Pitts, *The Houston Chronicle*, April 6, 2014.

147 See Matthew 22:30 and Galatians 3:28

148 www.progressive.org/magazine/meet-evangelist-tony-campolo/
Also see: www.redletterchristians.org/

149 The Gospel of John, 1:1–4, NRSV, excerpted

150 From my notes of a class lecture by Dr. Mallard at Candler School of Theology, ca. 1984.

151 Martin Luther, quoted by Alexander Chalmers, *The Table Talk of Martin Luther*, (1857), p.79.

152 Fred Hoyle, *Evolution from Space*, the Omni Lecture, Royal Institution, London, 12 January 1982.

153 Fred Hoyle, *The Intelligent Universe*, (Holt, Rinehart, and Winston, New York, 1984).

154 Fred Hoyle and N. Chandra Wickramasinghe, *Evolution from Space,* (J.M. Dent & Sons, London, 1981).

155 *Song of Myself,* Walt Whitman, in *Leaves of Grass*, (Boston: James R. Osgood & Co., 1881–82).

156 *Auguries of Innocence*, William Blake, in *The Pickering Manuscript* (1803).

157 Michael Talbot, *The Holographic Universe*, (New York: Harper Perennial, 2011), see pp. 47-48.

158 *The Atlantic*, November 7, and an article in *Quanta* magazine by Jennifer Ouellette www.theatlantic.com/science/archive/2016/11/quantum-brain/506768/and www.ncbi.nlm.nih.gov/pmc/articles/PMC5454345/ and
K. Harini K., Sowdhamini Sowdhamini, "Computational approaches for decoding select odorant-olfactory receptor interactions using mini-virtual screening," *PLOS One Journal*, July, 2015.

159 Cited from *Wired.com*, from original article in *Quanta*

magazine, August 1, 2013, by Peter Byrne, www.wired.
com/2013/08/quantum-biology/

160 *Matthew Henry Commentary of the Bible*, on the Scripture
passage Matthew 18:1–6.

161 Matthew 22:39

162 Galatians 5:6

163 Galatians 5:14

164 Matthew 6:33

165 Matthew 13:45–46, NKJV

Notes about Bible Quotations and Sources, and Bible Copyright Information

When Scriptures are fully identified within the body of my text
(using book, chapter and verse, such as, "John 3:16,") they may
not be footnoted here.

Scripture verses from the Holy Bible quoted herein are from
the New International Version (NIV), unless otherwise noted. In
a very few cases, I offer my own paraphrases from the Literal
Greek (from the Septuagint, using standard, interlinear Koine
Greek to English).

I try to avoid using "subjective" paraphrased versions,
instead using translations for accuracy and clarity of point. The
NIV is considered a more conservative/orthodox translation,
yet is widely recognized as very accurate and scholarly, even
though it does not use "inclusive language." I prefer inclusive
language (e.g., *humanity* rather than *mankind*) but I do not wish
to give fuel to Bible literalists who might accuse me of using only
"liberal" translations or of "cherry picking" verses or versions.
The NIV is a reliable choice otherwise.

Scripture quotations marked NIV are taken from the
Holy Bible, New International Version, ©1973, 1978, 1984 by
International Bible Society and Zondervan.

Scripture quotations marked AMP are from *The Amplified*

CIRCLE
BOOKS

CHRISTIAN FAITH

Circle Books explores a wide range of disciplines within the field
of Christian faith and practice. It also draws on personal testimony
and new ways of finding and expressing God's presence in the
world today.
If you have enjoyed this book, why not tell other readers by
posting a review on your preferred book site.

Recent bestsellers from Circle Books are:

I Am With You (Paperback)
John Woolley

These words of divine encouragement were given to John Woolley
in his work as a hospital chaplain, and have since inspired and
uplifted tens of thousands, even changed their lives.
Paperback: 978-1-90381-699-8 ebook: 978-1-78099-485-7

God Calling
A. J. Russell

365 messages of encouragement channelled from Christ to two
anonymous "Listeners".
Hardcover: 978-1-905047-42-0 ebook: 978-1-78099-486-4

The Long Road to Heaven
A Lent Course Based on the Film
Tim Heaton

This second Lent resource from the author of *The Naturalist and the
Christ* explores Christian understandings of "salvation" in a five-
part study based on the film *The Way*.
Paperback: 978-1-78279-274-1 ebook: 978-1-78279-273-4

Abide In My Love
More Divine Help for Today's Needs
John Woolley

The companion to *I Am With You, Abide In My Love* offers words of
divine encouragement.
Paperback: 978-1-84694-276-1

From the Bottom of the Pond
The Forgotten Art of Experiencing God in the Depths of the
Present Moment
Simon Small
From the Bottom of the Pond takes us into the depths of the present
moment, to the only place where God can be found.
Paperback: 978-1-84694-066-8 ebook: 978-1-78099-207-5

God Is A Symbol Of Something True
Why You Don't Have to Choose Either a Literal Creator God or a
Blind, Indifferent Universe
Jack Call
In this examination of modern spiritual dilemmas, Call offers the
explanation that some of the most important elements of life are
beyond our control: everything is fundamentally alright.
Paperback: 978-1-84694-244-0

The Scarlet Cord
Conversations With God's Chosen Women
Lindsay Hardin Freeman, Karen N. Canton
Voiceless wax figures no longer, twelve biblical women,
outspoken, independent, faithful, selfless risk-takers, come to life
in *The Scarlet Cord*.
Paperback: 978-1-84694-375-1

Will You Join in Our Crusade?
The Invitation of the Gospels Unlocked by the Inspiration of Les
Miserables
Steve Mann
Les Miserables' narrative is entwined with Bible study in this book
of 42 daily readings from the Gospels, perfect for Lent or anytime.
Paperback: 978-1-78279-384-7 ebook: 978-1-78279-383-0

A Quiet Mind
Uniting Body, Mind and Emotions in Christian Spirituality
Eva McIntyre
A practical guide to finding peace in the present moment that will
change your life, heal your wounds and bring you a quiet mind.
Paperback: 978-1-84694-507-6 ebook: 978-1-78099-005-7

Readers of ebooks can buy or view any of these bestsellers by
clicking on the live link in the title. Most titles are published in
paperback and as an ebook. Paperbacks are available in traditional
bookshops. Both print and ebook formats are available online.

Find more titles and sign up to our readers' newsletter at
http://www.johnhuntpublishing.com/christianity. Follow us on
Facebook at https://www.facebook.com/ChristianAlternative.